T0248157

Praise for *Journey to Eloheh*

"Randy and Edith Woodley write with insight and wisdom from their years of experience. They have prophetic voices that draw attention to the needs of all of our relatives. Their voices rise out of difficult situations in which they have done more than survive; they are showing how to flourish in an ever-changing world."

—**Ray Aldred**, director of the Indigenous Studies Program, Vancouver School of Theology

"A practical antidote to despair, hopelessness, and aimless consumption, this book offers a robust and healing path to well-being for all of us. The Woodleys are wise and trustworthy guides for restoration and embodied goodness within the community of creation."

—**Sarah Bessey**, author of *Field Notes for the Wilderness: Practices for an Evolving Faith*

"Spiritual journey as autobiography: like a Navajo weaver, *Journey to Eloheh* skillfully connects Native American theology and personal experience into a way of life. If you are looking for your own path, Edith and Randy Woodley's story is a good place to begin."

—**Steven Charleston**, author of *Ladder to the Light*, *Spirit Wheel*, and *We Survived the End of the World*

"Edith and Randy Woodley's passion and persistence to create spaces of community and care are inspiring. A blend of storytelling, theology, and guidance harvested directly through Indigenous wisdom, *Journey to Eloheh* reminds us to stay true to the path of kinship and belonging, and to never give up on justice and peacemaking in the world. I highly recommend this book for anyone who is searching for a way to be a better relative on this earth or to fight for a better reality for future generations. This book will help you get there."

—**Kaitlin B. Curtice**, award-winning author of *Native* and *Living Resistance*

"In my twenty-seven-year journey as a pastor, I had two prolonged, intense internal struggles wrestling to keep my faith. Randy and Edith Woodley's Indigenous values and their friendship played big parts in restoring hope for me during my second struggle. Their generous sharing of painfully beautiful and vulnerable stories, along with life-giving, wise values, in *Journey to Eloheh* will surely be a gift to anyone who reads it."

—**Eddie Han**, pastor in Los Angeles

"For many years, I have considered Randy Woodley one of my teachers. His books, lectures, and personal conversations—together with his humble, yet bold, spirit as a teacher—have enriched and challenged me. His new book, co-written with his wise and eloquent wife, Edith, is a masterpiece, a book I would recommend to anyone and everyone. It beautifully combines the sharing of their life-story with the essence of their lifeway, articulated in ten powerful Indigenous values that are as deeply spiritual as they are deeply practical."

—**Brian McLaren**, author, teacher, and activist

"There is so much we can all learn from the wisdom of Indigenous culture. In this book, Randy and Edith Woodley invite us to join them on a journey of learning a different way of living that leads to wholeness, abundance, and peace. They generously share their life experience and spiritual insights to show us a better path toward harmony with the whole of creation. I highly recommend it!"

—**Dr. Brenda Salter McNeil,** author of *Becoming Brave* and *Roadmap to Reconciliation 2.0*

"Being Native Hawaiian and growing up in the continental United States, I found the ten Indigenous values Randy and Edith Woodley talk about in their book resonating deeply in my soul. I have deep ancestral roots in Lahaina, and it is these Indigenous values that are sustaining my families as they face the future rebuilding of their homes and historical Lahaina Town after the wildfire. In *Journey to Eloheh*, Randy and Edith share from personal vulnerabilities and challenges in their journey."

—**Jim Sequeira,** pastor and facilitator, Journey to Mosaic and racial righteousness

JOURNEY TO ELOHEH

JOURNEY TO ELOHEH

HOW INDIGENOUS VALUES LEAD US TO HARMONY AND WELL-BEING

RANDY AND EDITH WOODLEY

Broadleaf Books
Minneapolis

JOURNEY TO ELOHEH
How Indigenous Values Lead Us to Harmony and Well-Being

29 28 27 26 25 24   1 2 3 4 5 6 7 8 9

Library of Congress Cataloging-in-Publication Data

Names: Woodley, Randy, author. | Woodley, Edith, author.
Title: Journey to Eloheh : how indigenous values lead us to
    harmony and well-being / Randy and Edith Woodley.
Other titles: How indigenous values lead us to harmony and
    well-being
Description: Minneapolis, MN : Broadleaf Books, [2024] | Includes
    bibliographical references. Identifiers: LCCN 2023053498
    (print) | LCCN 2023053499 (ebook) | ISBN 9781506496979
    (print) | ISBN 9781506496986 (ebook)
Subjects: LCSH: Indian philosophy—North America. | Harmony
    (Philosophy) | Woodley, Randy | Woodley, Edith
Classification: LCC E98.P5 W65 2024 (print) | LCC E98.P5
    (ebook) | DDC 108.997—dc23/eng/20240212
LC record available at https://lccn.loc.gov/2023053498
LC ebook record available at https://lccn.loc.gov/2023053499

Cover image: © 2023 Shutterstock; Set of colorful watercolor hand painted circle isolated on white. Watercolor illustration for artistic design. Round stains, blobs of burgundy, brown, dark red, sienna, rufous, maroon color/669459781 by Katsiaryna Chumakova
Cover design: Studio Gearbox

Print ISBN: 978-1-5064-9697-9
eBook ISBN: 978-1-5064-9698-6

Printed in China.

For Joe and Billie Engavo:
your determination, support, and dedication have been a lifeline!

CONTENTS

Do not begrudge the white man for coming here.
Though he doesn't know it yet,
he has come to learn from us.

—A Shoshone elder

INTRODUCTION

The Search for Happiness

Most self-help books aim to help readers find happiness. They may be about losing weight or making money or finding the love of your life. They might even go a bit deeper and offer to help you find purpose, meaning, and spiritual fulfillment. But ultimately, those books target readers who long to be happier than they are now—and who are willing to shell out twenty bucks for a book that promises to help them. Browse at any bookstore or online retailer, and you will have lots of books to choose from.

This is not one of those books. Our story is not about how we found happiness by following a five-step plan. It's not about helping you manifest your own individual dreams or find your purpose. Happiness, in our contemporary society, has come to mean a state of feeling good. When people talk about happiness, they often mean feeling comfortable, at ease, fulfilled, entertained, and successful. "We just want you to be happy," many people say to their children. "You both look so happy!" people say to a new couple.

The pursuit of happiness tracks a long history in the United States. It is embedded right there in the Declaration of Independence, listed as one of the three "unalienable rights" that the founders say Creator gives to all human beings: life, liberty, and the pursuit of happiness. While we can't know exactly what the framers of the Declaration of Independence meant by those words, we *can* know who they thought possessed those rights—and who didn't. Thomas Jefferson and his peers didn't think of the "merciless Indian savages," whom they mention later in the declaration, as human beings possessing those rights. Nor did they include enslaved Black people in that group of humans, given that forty-one of the fifty-six signers were slaveholders. Apparently, life, liberty, and the pursuit of happiness weren't for everyone. Forgive us if we're not excited about whatever brand of happiness they claimed some people—and not others—had the right to pursue!

This book is about creating *well-being*, which is very different from seeking one's own private happiness and definitely different from the sort of happiness those enslavers had in mind. People describe a sense of well-being with various words: *health, wholeness, harmony, shalom, right living*, or even *the common good*. Well-being is a much more inclusive pursuit than happiness, one that is concerned about the wholeness and thriving of others—and not just other people but everything in our environment. Well-being, as we are describing it, is for all.

When the two of us (Edith and Randy) talk about well-being, we mean a way of living that includes the whole community of creation. It's a way of living that emerges from Indigenous lifeways, as we will see—values passed down from those very "merciless Indian savages" who the founders did not view as possessing a right to life, liberty, and the pursuit of happiness. Native people know that we as humans are intimately related to all living things. We are in a reciprocal relationship with every other being—and so are you! If you are not well, how can I be? If our rivers are not experiencing well-being, how can we? If our mountains are not well, how can the land below them, and the people on that land, thrive?

Measures of well-being must also include the way our society operates in all its systems and structures from small businesses to large corporations, small social gatherings to large movements, and small governments to large nation-states—including all the customs, rules, and laws that govern them. It's like happiness and well-being are made up of two different substances: one is composed of personal satisfaction, and one of communal, even planetary, good. In short, when we talk about well-being, we are concerned with the well-being of *all*.

So while we don't want to split hairs, we must remember that *happiness* and *well-being* are two different things entirely. Happiness may be a byproduct of well-being, but it is not the prime product or even the aim. Western definitions of happiness—and Western maps of how you get there—may even lead you *away* from well-being. Individual success, private comfort, career advancement, wealth building: research shows that the things that we think will make us happy usually don't. Humans are not always good forecasters of what will actually bring us a sense of happiness or well-being.

Indeed, many of the values held by the Western world run *contrary* to living well. For example, the Western worldview stresses individualism over the good of the whole community. The Western worldview—which descends from the settlers who landed on this continent—emphasizes competition over cooperation. If you seek to live in harmony—to find true well-being—using only the values available to you through the Western worldview, you are much like the fellow who got lost on the back roads of Maine. He stopped and asked an old man sitting on his porch how to get to a particular city. With his Maine brogue intact, the old man answered, "Ya can't get there from here."

Maybe you feel a bit lost, too, having tried all the roads to happiness and still not having found your way. Or maybe you're realizing that you've had the wrong destination in mind all along. Perhaps you're finding out that the road to what you used to call happiness is a road toward a precipice: of social decay, planetary catastrophe, and personal alienation, depression, and despair. Maybe you know now that the place you long to arrive looks less like happiness and more like well-being. And possibly you're realizing that you can't get there using the values contained in the map that your parents, friends, social media, and advertisers have handed to you.

So, if you are no longer sure that you can get there from here, what can you do?

The Harmony Way

We will be speaking of the Harmony Way throughout this entire journey. Native Americans and most other Indigenous peoples around the world consider a Harmony Way of well-being as the foundation of their societies.* In the Cherokee language, this concept of well-being is often called *Eloheh* (pronounced ay-luh-HAY).

The Cherokee meaning of well-being is deep and resonant, and it is hard to capture in English. *Eloheh* means "well-being," yes, but it means so much more. Eloheh—what some traditions call the Harmony Way—describes a state of being when all is as it should be or as it was created

---

* We use several terms to represent the Indigenous peoples in what is now known as North America. Words such as *Indian, American Indian, Native American, First Nations,* and *American Aboriginal* are all socially constructed words referring to the earliest inhabitants of Turtle Island (America). America's original or host peoples would most often prefer to be called by their specific tribal name. But we live in a time when words like *Native American* and *White* and *Asian* and others all have social meaning. We will use most of these terms for Indigenous peoples interchangeably throughout the book. Also, the terms *Harmony Way* and *Eloheh* will be used interchangeably.

to be. Eloheh means that people are at peace, not at war; that the Earth is being cared for and producing in abundance, so no one goes hungry. Eloheh means people are treating each other fairly and that no one is a stranger for very long.

Eloheh is a word that we as a couple have related to for more than three decades. It's the word we have chosen as a reference point in raising our family. Eloheh is at the center of our service to our community, and it encompasses the values in which we have built community over the years. So when we share our journey to Eloheh, know that we are speaking in the broadest of terms and the most intimate as well. We are talking about overall well-being but with very specific applications. We will share more later about the actual word *Eloheh*.

We have been on this journey to Eloheh for quite some time. For many years, people have listened to us, read our books, and visited Eloheh Indigenous Center for Earth Justice, our regenerative agroecology farm in Oregon. For years, people have asked us to write our story. Finally, we have decided it is time.

I (Edith) am an artist, activist, farmer, and Eastern Shoshone tribal member raised on the Wind River Indian Reservation in Wyoming. My father was a survivor of an Indian boarding school. I (Randy) am an activist, farmer, scholar, teacher, and Cherokee descendant, recognized by the Keetoowah Band. You'll read our individual stories later in the book. When you do so, you will begin to understand how the most broken, abused, and fragmented people can be healed through an Eloheh journey.

Our stories are unique to us, just as your story is partic-
ular to you. We each come from very different lifestyles and
environments. We are finding well-being for ourselves day
by day. We are pretty sure we are not the prime examples of
harmony and well-being! But we *have* learned some things
along the way, and we really can't tell someone else's journey
anyway. So, we hope that our stories will demonstrate that
regardless of our unique origins, we can all find our way to
a good life with others. The high value we place on diversity
has helped us craft a life together. As simple human beings
trying to live in a good way, we all have much in common.

In this story, we will highlight other values in addition
to diversity—values needed to live harmoniously with the
whole community of creation. The ten values we will share
in this book compose what you could think of as Eloheh's
core values. Taken together, these values create a path
toward true well-being—a Harmony Way.

Some might wonder whether Eloheh is a philosophy or
even a religion. We think about the Harmony Way as a
lifeway. The values of the Harmony Way become both the
destination toward which we're headed and the journey we
take to get there.

Ten Eloheh Values

The ten values we will focus on in this book are harmony,
respect, accountability, history, humor, authenticity, equal-
ity, community, balance, and generosity. These same values
have been foundational for many Indigenous societies. We

will show how these values, and their connected practices, have shown up among our Indian people and in our lives.

Indigenous peoples everywhere have tested these values from time immemorial. We don't claim to know everything about all Indigenous nations and tribes. We don't even claim that there are only ten important shared values; we can speak only from what we discovered on our own journey. Also, we acknowledge these ten values have never created perfect societies. Yet they have shaped societies in such a way that, for the most part, people learned to live well with the Earth, with the whole community of creation, and even with people who are very different from themselves.

How do we know that these Eloheh values have sustained millions of Indigenous peoples for thousands of years? For one, we have been deeply involved in dozens of Native American tribal communities over the years. Here on Turtle Island (North America), we have seen Indigenous people putting these same values into practice repeatedly. We have also had the good fortune of spending time with Indigenous peoples from around the globe, and those people have affirmed to us that these same values form the basis of their own societies.

You may wonder: How could Indigenous peoples all over the Earth share similar values? There are several answers. The simplest explanation is that the Earth herself has been the common teacher. Indigenous people, by necessity of survival, have learned to thrive on every part of the planet because they learned to live with the Earth. They allowed themselves to be taught by her. Second, these societies have been around much longer than our modern nation-states have. Over time, Indigenous peoples have learned what values they need to sustain themselves well into the future.

Perhaps you are the type of person who needs evidence. You want data: proof that these values are what has sustained so many Indigenous societies for so many millennia. If that's you, I (Randy) can provide research-backed claims. For my PhD work, I queried forty-five tribes across nearly every region of the United States and Canada, and I interviewed a dozen spiritual leaders and elders. Through that process, I was able to verify that these ten common values undergird the cultures of all those tribes. In addition, I verified these values unofficially through conversations with international classmates and other friends who were Hawaiians; Māori from New Zealand; Aboriginals from Australia; Saami from Scandinavia; Ikalahan Filipino; Maasai from Samburu, Kenya; Zulu from South Africa; and others. They all share a way of living that sees harmony as foundational, and they ascribe to most, if not all, of these ten values.

Reading this book will introduce you to these ten Indigenous values and a more Indigenous worldview. It will help you understand the many meanings behind the idea of Eloheh, and it will help you distinguish the Harmony Way from the false happiness promised by so many people who want our money. We hope a whole new world will open up to you as you discover your relatedness to the rest of the community of creation. You will also come to understand your foundational purpose as a human being along the way.

First, we will examine the very real way that Western values have brought us to the edge of a precipice as a species. Then, the two of us will share the journeys that have brought us to this place. After that, we will look in some detail at each of the ten Indigenous values that help us live in a good way, find true well-being, and live in harmony with the whole community of creation. Throughout the book, you will learn about some Indigenous history, story, ceremony, and practice, too. Because you can't learn a people's values without learning about their history and daily lives.

Welcome to the journey to Eloheh.

PART I

MOVING TOWARD THE PRECIPICE

1

A DISTORTED REALITY

How False Binaries Came to Be

You may have heard the saying that opinions are like navels: everybody has one, and they are all different.

Facts—or what we *think* are facts—can be much the same as opinions. As we are shaped by the society around us, we begin to understand certain things as normal and even true. At one point, people living in European cultures thought the world was flat. That was considered a fact. The church considered any opinion contrary to that "fact" to be heresy, and you could be persecuted for holding a contrary belief.

We generally talk about *culture* as those taken-for-granted artifacts and practices shared by a group. Culture is composed of things that can be observed. *Worldview* goes much deeper than culture, although it intersects with culture. Worldview—simply, how we see the world—is basically what we "know" to be true. Our worldview includes what we consider to be normal. Here's an example: cultural differences include things such as whether we eat sliced bread made from wheat or Ethiopian injera made from teff. Worldview differences include how we *think* about bread and how we view the role of food in general. Worldview refers to the intangible but very real way a people group understand, for example, a food's relationship to life.

At one time, social scientists believed that people's worldviews could not be changed. They thought our worldviews were as fixed as our skin color or our hair. As a result of globalization, however, they have changed their minds. In other words, the world is no longer flat. Social scientists now generally agree that not only can people change their worldviews but they can even operate from two different worldviews *simultaneously*. (Anthropologists call someone who can operate with multiple worldviews Indigenous cosmopolitans. It's a fancy term that just means we can possess multiple worldviews.)

As you learn the how and why of another worldview, you learn not just how to *act* in the culture but how to *think* differently. That worldviews are not immutable shouldn't surprise anyone. Marginalized people have had to learn to think from multiple worldviews for millennia. Women have had to think from both male and female worldviews for ages; enslaved people have had to figure out the enslaver's worldview just to survive; and Indigenous people long ago figured out how to stay alive by understanding the settlers' worldview.

If you are not immersed in a Native American community, it may be difficult to understand just how distinctive a Native American worldview is from a Western worldview. At first glance, contemporary Native Americans live in similar houses, drive similar vehicles, wear similar clothes, and often eat similar food to the descendants of settlers and others. But the worldview of America's Indigenous peoples was formed in radically different directions from the worldview of Western Europeans. That distinction may be invisible, but that doesn't mean it doesn't exist.

The hopeful thing here is that if worldviews can be changed, so can culture. Over time, we can begin to shift our worldview. We can stop seeing the world as flat and start seeing it as round—we've already done that. We can stop viewing the world as a simple resource and start seeing it as a community of creation. We can stop chasing happiness and start nurturing well-being. The journey to Eloheh involves switching out one worldview for another. This trade is necessary if we are all going to live well—and just survive—into the future.

Before we look at the ten Indigenous values that offer hope for real well-being, we need to look briefly at the Western worldview that has gotten us into this mess and the ways in which it is distinct from a Native worldview.

What Is the Western Worldview?

The first thing we should note is that the Western world-view has affected us all. With the advent of empire came colonization. Colonization in the West meant taking on the values that promote and maintain empire. In a sense, we are all being held captive to the way of empire and the systems created by empire.

There is a direct line from colonization to the everyday ills among Native Americans. Colonization has been one of the greatest health risks to Native Americans. Colonization is a sickness from which Native Americans and others must be delivered and healed. The path to better health, wellness, or well-being for Native Americans is decolonization and re-indiginization: to peel back the layers of the false myths and narratives we have been told, to hear from those who have differing stories, and to become intimately acquainted with the land. Non-Natives must go through a similar process.

It's important to note here that there are non-Native people who hold a more Indigenous worldview, and there are Native Americans who hold a more Western worldview. But the exceptions, in some way, prove the rule. In general, the worldview developed in the West—no matter who holds it—is taking us on a journey that leads away from well-being.

In my book *Shalom and the Community of Creation: An Indigenous Vision*, I (Randy) lay out a chart that reveals some of the differences between a Euro-American Western worldview and a Native American worldview. On a pie chart reflecting a Western worldview, beliefs take up nearly all the space, whereas in an Indigenous worldview, few if any beliefs do not involve a practice. In other words, Indigenous practices themselves function as beliefs. In Native thought, how you *live* is seen as what you believe. I asked an elder once about his beliefs. He replied, "I believe on being a good husband, father, grandfather, and a good person in helping my community. I believe in being kind to people, especially strangers. I believe in practicing my ceremonies; those are my beliefs."

But in a Western worldview, there can be and often is a wide gap between what one *believes* and what one *practices*. Those who hold a Western worldview see correct beliefs as being of primary importance.

Consider for a moment how many people in the history of Christianity, especially in North Africa and Europe, were excommunicated or even killed because of their religious *beliefs*. Bishops gathered on numerous occasions to excommunicate other bishops over their beliefs. Sometimes these Christian councils even silenced their opposition by putting them to death. Christians killed Muslims during the Crusades, Protestants killed Roman Catholics and vice versa, some Christians killed Anabaptists and other Protestants with differing doctrinal beliefs. (Didn't Jesus teach his followers to love their enemies, not kill them?)

In the land we now call America, prior to European contact, there was never a war based on people's understanding of religion. Let that fact sink in. Indigenous groups waged wars, yes—but never over religious belief. Murdering those who have differing religious beliefs continues in the West even to the modern era, but why? Why do some Christians consider beliefs to be worth fighting and even killing over?

This question is quite complicated, and answering it would require analyzing over twenty-five hundred years of world history. We can't do that in this book. What is important is to know that Western Europeans came to value reason over experience. For them, there was a difference between what was considered objective reality (that which is observable) and subjective reality (that which we know through experience).

When people invest themselves in a split reality, their thoughts and theologies can easily become disembodied. In such a worldview, everything physical—the land, good works, our bodies—becomes suspect. Another way Western religion captures this false reality is by believing that the God of the universe is at work *only* in their own religion or even their own congregation. This creates a secular-sacred split.

The American Puritans especially exhibited this split. One of the premier Puritan theologians, Cotton Mather, said after the massacre of residents of a friendly Pequot village: "In a little more than one hour, five or six hundred of these barbarians were dismissed from a world that was burdened with them. It may be demanded. . . . Should not Christians have more mercy and compassion? But . . . sometimes the Scripture declareth women and children must perish with their parents. . . . We had sufficient light from the word of God for our proceedings."

Such a split—a deadly one, as it turns out, for Native Americans—was reinforced through what is called *binary thinking*. In binary thinking, Puritans and others operating from that worldview judged everything to be either right or wrong, with no middle ground. Other examples of binary thinking include legal or illegal, heaven or hell, sin or holiness, success or failure, civilized or primitive, introvert or extrovert, saved or lost, clean or dirty, weeds or plants. This type of absolutism makes it difficult for Western thinkers to hold two seemingly incompatible things in tension without having to find a resolution.

In a Western worldview, growing out of perspectives in ancient Greece, individual authority also became much more important than community authority. And reason would always triumph, meaning that people thought all problems could be solved by educated men.[†] Binary thinking also creates the false assumption that all things can be understood and every problem can be solved. This hubris birthed a sense of superiority, which often translated into the idea of a superior nation, ethnic group, or race.

Of course, people who hold the Western worldview have always understood themselves to belong to the highest form of civilization—more advanced than people in what they considered more primitive states, such as Native Americans. As time marched on, this sense of superiority was reinforced. This is the myth of *progressive civilization*, about which Seneca elder and scholar John Mohawk comments,

---

†   "Men" here is meant to represent males, not all humanity.

"For the most part, contemporary historians have proceeded from the presumption that modern people are different from and superior to those who came before—especially those designated as 'primitives.' . . . These accounts serve to reinforce the sense of difference and to distance moderns from unflattering legacies of the past."

The truth of history is that the Western worldview—which, in America, included a powerful colonizing force called Christian religion—promises future hope, salvation, development, security, and a higher form of civilization. What the Western worldview has delivered, however, especially to Indigenous peoples, is imbalance, oppression, violence, and the destruction of people, creatures, and land—what we call the whole community of creation. Before the arrival of European settler colonialism, Native America was much healthier, more tolerant of diversity, and more in tune with the environment than were European societies.

Binary thinking remains alive and well in all sectors of modern society, whether religion, education, politics, economics, or the judicial system. The problems of our dualistic systems are manifold, including, for example, laws that do not provide equal protection for women. White male supremacy—meaning the belief that White men of European descent deserve to oversee all systems—is at the root of this thinking. In religion, the most obvious culprit is disembodied theologies that emphasize correct beliefs over correct practices. Simply put, Native Americans never embraced that split in reality.

Distinctions

Now let's look at some of the differences between a Western worldview and a Native American one. The following comparison between the worldviews of Native Americans and Western Europeans may help to illustrate some of the major differences. (While it might seem like we're setting up a false binary here, it's important to note that we can compare two things without falling into dualism. There are natural and unnatural binaries.) Again, most of our understanding in this area was constructed through our years of traveling among various North American tribal peoples and through my (Randy's) PhD dissertation. While this chart distills these two worldviews down to essentials that do not fit every person or community living within them, they help us understand, in general ways, the differences between the two.

Western European–Based Worldview	Native North American Worldview
physically dualistic	physically holistic
morally dualistic	morally holistic
essentially ethereal (spiritual)	tangible spirituality
religiously intolerant (force-fix)	life governed by harmony
individualistic	community is essential
extrinsically categorical	relationally categorical
hierarchical	egalitarian (with exceptions)
humor reserved for nonspiritual	humor is sacred and necessary
based on competitive greed	based on cooperative consensus

force or war wins	negotiation and peacemaking
based in utopia	based in this world
White supremacist	diversity gives strength
words are not binding	words have primordial power
work in order to work	purposeful and meaningful work
anthropocentric	people as a relative to all creation
triumphalist	humility a strong virtue
greed-based	generosity a strong virtue
patriarchal	women as important as men
inhospitable	hospitality a strong virtue

Understanding our own worldview is a vital starting point on the journey to Eloheh. The most important points for us to remember are these: First, worldview is passed down to all of us initially, without choice, but worldviews can be changed. Second, worldview is not invented in each generation or even individually; it is constructed over centuries. Third, we generally only notice our own worldview when confronted with a different way of thinking or with another worldview. Fourth, a split in reality, such as in the European-American worldview, is a false binary, not based on the whole of reality. Fifth, systems such as religion, philosophy, education, politics, law, criminal justice, economics, and others that are a part of our everyday reality are built on false assumptions wrought through a false reality. These false realities have costs. To live into the whole of reality, we must adopt a worldview that is more holistic.

Living within a false reality has consequences. One of the critical ways that the Western worldview has failed is our treatment of the Earth and the whole community of creation. We prefer to think of the *planet*—something separate from us—as being in trouble. But in reality, we, the human species, are the ones in grave danger.

In the end, we believe the Earth will recover from the ravages of human-induced climate change. We just hope *we* as a species can change our worldviews and actions in time. What will it take for us as humans to survive and sustain harmony here?

2

A FAILED EXPERIMENT

How the West Was Lost

Climate change: **those two** words should scare any reasonable person. Climate change gives us a sense of dread, insecurity, and loss of control. Mental health professionals are seeing more and more clients who struggle with climate anxiety: a sense of fear and despair in the face of planetary catastrophe.

Way back in 1912, a New Zealand newspaper ran an article titled "Coal Consumption Affecting Climate." In it, a scientist reports, "The furnaces of the world are now burning about 2 [billion] tons of coal a year. When this is burned, uniting with oxygen, it adds about 7 [billion] tons of carbon dioxide to the atmosphere yearly. This tends to make the air a more effective blanket for the Earth and to raise its temperature. The effect may be considerable in a few centuries."

The term *greenhouse gases* was first used even earlier, back in 1896, by a Swedish scientist named Svante Arrhenius. In a paper published that year, he made an early calculation of how much warmer the Earth was becoming, thanks to the energy-trapping nature of some of the gases in the atmosphere. Even at this early stage, he understood that humans had the potential to play a significant role in changing the concentration of at least one of those gases, carbon dioxide (known as "carbonic acid" back then).

So, more than one hundred years ago, scientists knew that the climate was being changed by humans. But the tipping point came sooner than they expected. Today, CO_2 is being released into the atmosphere faster than at any time in the past sixty-six million years. And apparently, we refuse to stop.

We can't talk about well-being without talking about the home that sustains us. And you can't understand our journey—in particular, how we ended up calling ourselves co-sustainers of Eloheh Indigenous Center for Earth Justice and Eloheh Farm & Seeds—without talking about the urgency of climate change. Climate-related disasters now occur frequently and in all parts of the world. These so-called natural disasters caused us to dig deep in our own everyday practices and to seriously ask ourselves: What role will we play in shaping the future for the following generations?

When we say we are moving toward a precipice, it is both a metaphor and our literal reality. The precipice is real. The journey toward Eloheh may be the only way to back away from the edge of our own extinction.

In this chapter we'll look at how the West was lost. If the Western worldview was a failed experiment in conquest, domination, and imperial fantasy, how might we begin to shed its influence and adopt a different worldview? How might we act differently? We'll also look at how the natural world might teach us about adaptation, diversity, and hope.

A New Epoch

Many scientists say we are living in the *Anthropocene*: a geological age in which humans (*anthro*) have had a substantial, dominant influence on nature. Will Steffen of the Climate Change Institute of Australian National University says that we can consider the advent of the Anthropocene as either 1800 (the Industrial Revolution) or 1950 (the atomic age). Either way, he says, the new name will serve as "a strong reminder to the general public that we are now having undeniable impacts on the environment at the scale of the planet as a whole, so much so that a new geological epoch has begun."

In other words, calling our era the *Anthropocene* reminds us that humanity created this mess.

And that's true—partially. But let's not lay the responsibility of climate change on *all* humans, since not all humans have influenced nature negatively. That's like making the whole class stay in from recess and calling them delinquents because two kids have been acting up. Professor Jairus Grove at the University of Hawaii pinpoints *which* humans have caused the most damage. He describes why he chooses the term *Eurocene* instead of *Anthropocene*:

> It was a European elite that developed a distinctively mechanistic view of matter, an oppositional relationship to nature, and an economic system indebted to geographical expansion. The resulting political orders measured success by how much wealth could be generated in the exploitation of peoples and resources. The geological record bears the mark of this European assemblage of hierarchies. Understanding the forces of Europeanization—the forces of racial superiority, economic hegemony, and global resettlement—is essential to understanding how the planet got to this point.

No one is above bias, including scientists. Vandana Shiva, an Indian scholar and environmental activist, says that modern science has a worldview that both supports and is supported by the sociopolitical-economic system of Western capitalist patriarchy, which dominates and exploits nature, women, and the poor.

Shiva believes science is influenced by what she calls sociopolitical-economic factors, including patriarchy. The patriarchal elite, with their Western worldview, wield their power in certain ways. There is a parallel relationship between how they regard nature and how they treat people. Ecofeminist Rosemary Radford Ruether states, "Women must see that there can be no liberation for them and no solution to the ecological crisis within a society whose fundamental model of relationships continues to be one of domination." Similarly, Shiva points out, "We are either going to have a future where women lead the way to make peace with the Earth or we are not going to have a human future at all."

Notice that Grove's term *Eurocene* situates the blame on the European elite—and remember that this elite was predominantly male. European Americans, operating from a Western worldview, treat the natural world and the people they can dominate in similar ways. This is true especially concerning women. It's also true concerning the cultural, racial, gendered, and immigrant Other, as well as the poor, White or otherwise. The common goals of elite European and American patriarchal systems of oppression have always been to control, objectify, gain pleasure from, expect production from, and exploit. The sense of superiority over the Earth and people is uncanny.

We don't think it is fair to blame all of humanity for climate change. And we realize we all share a worldview that has been influenced and even dominated by men, especially when it comes to wielding power. We choose to call our era the *Europatricene*: a geological era dominated and determined by White European–based men.

Living out Indigenous values in the Europatricene isn't easy, as it requires us to go against every force that shapes us: advertising, social media, commerce, pop culture, and political assumptions. But standing on the precipice of human history, poised on the edge of extinguishment, we have no other choice.

How Bad Is It?

At the risk of providing a litany of horrors, let's examine some of the problems facing us in the Europatricene. The "faster, bigger, cheaper" approach to food is draining the Earth's resources dry and destroying our health. The Earth's topsoil is depleting at more than 13 percent the rate it can be replaced. We have already lost 75–95 percent of the world's crop varieties over the last century. Over the past ten years, we've had one hundred million tons of herbicides dumped onto our crops, polluting our soil and streams. Genetically engineered crops are now speeding up the destructive process by completely altering the composition of soil bacteria in the fields where such crops are grown.

Indeed, the Western worldview has devised ways to intentionally aid us in forgetting how to live *with* and care *for* creation. This calculated forgetfulness leads to the marks of a bad relationship. Topsoil is disappearing. Forests are shrinking. Desertification is advancing. Coral reefs are dying. Plants, fish, insects, birds, and animal species are going extinct.

And water, that essential element of life: even as sea levels rise and there's increased flooding, our freshwater supply is disappearing. The key to understanding freshwater supply is understanding cycles and seasons. When the natural cycles of rain and snow distribution are disrupted, they bring too much water in one place and not enough in another. When people begin disrupting these natural cycles, even by damming a river, we are playing a very dangerous game, and nature will always win. So where did all the water go? The world's water supplies are retained and available to us through snow melt, rain, and in aquifers. Snow and rain are on a general decline, and we are draining our aquifers dry as droughts increase.

Think about the connection of water to food. The average person drinks about four liters of water daily, in various forms. But the water used to produce our daily food equals about two thousand liters. Big Agriculture, with its factory farming and overuse of irresponsible irrigation systems, uses about 70 percent of all the world's water. The second greatest use comes from industry, at about 20 percent. Residential use is a mere 10 percent. Connect the dots: with competition increasing in all three sectors, water shortages translate to food shortages. Big Ag can't save us from itself.

But there is hope. The United Nations did a study showing that small farms can feed the world. Small farms are more adaptable. They are less costly, because they don't need extremely expensive machinery, and less environmentally damaging, because they don't need to spray chemicals. And they provide greater local economic opportunities than large industrial farms do. Small farms have been proven to produce higher yields per acre and more nutrient-dense foods. It is no accident that a key component on our land at Eloheh is a small teaching farm that demonstrates these principles.

A Brief History of Empire

What happened? How did we reach this precipice? How did we come to be peering into a future with a devastated climate and an uninhabitable planet?

The story is long and complex, but historically, it follows unjust empires as they expanded their reach. As empires misuse their own native land, water, and people, they go in search of more of the same to conquer. They irresponsibly feed these resources from the colonies to the beast. Like locusts, empires eventually destroy everything in their paths. At the same time when they are colonizing the land, they are colonizing people, through unjust means such as genocide and slavery. And empires do not just colonize people's bodies; they are also hard at work colonizing people's minds. Thus, their subjects often begin to hold an imperial worldview, like the one promoted by the empire.

Take England and parts of Western Europe, for example. When America was "discovered," much of Western Europe was in trouble. While feeding the fires of war, the Europeans also fed literal fires, to smelt iron for weapons of war. Also in high production were iron tools and timber, which were needed to build castles, fortresses, and cathedrals. For such a process, hardwood trees, such as native oaks, were needed for smelting fires. Oak forests were logged, overused, and depleted.

What were some of the first exports from what would become the United States? Virgin American oak trees. Deforestation was a reality in England and other Western European nations, and those colonizers passed on the problem to those they colonized. Extractive models prevailed in creating a very bad relationship between those particular humans and the rest of the community of creation.

Many European nations shared other maladies in addition to deforestation and war. Already in those centuries, with deforestation being a major contributor, European nations had caused topsoil depletion, and their oceans and bays were becoming polluted and fished-out. Rivers and streams had become undrinkable, and air pollution made breathing unhealthy. Disease was killing tens of thousands of people, and large mammals were going extinct. Classism reigned, cities became overcrowded, and the majority of people lived in poverty. Corruption and greed ran rampant, and injustice became the norm except for the top 1 percent.

Sound familiar? These are all the same ills that we on Turtle Island are now experiencing. These problems, embedded within a failed worldview, traveled here with the Europeans. Because of their extreme hubris, settlers believed they were superior to Native Americans. They insisted on duplicating a dangerous worldview based on a false reality. And here we all now live, in the Europatricene, staring down a possible future of our own species' demise.

Native Americans attempted to hold on to a more holistic and less invasive view of reality. The Indigenous peoples of Turtle Island likely spent centuries learning from the land and developing sustainable values. After more than 530 years of the Western worldview in America, we think it is fair to call the Western worldview a failed experiment. Western civilization has done Turtle Island and the world little good, and it has caused damage beyond compare.

Some foundational truths of the universe have been lost to a dualistic, patriarchal Western worldview. The first is how we view our relationship with the Earth—although our current state of connection is likely too anemic to describe with the word *relationship*. To be in true relationship with someone is not just about proximity; we all walk on the Earth. But how do we *relate* to Mother Earth? Currently, much of humanity's relationship with the Earth— what we call the whole community of creation—is quite narcissistic. Instead of caring for and tending to the relationship with the rest of creation, as a whole we, like abusers in relationship with their victims, seem to care only about ourselves.

But we are not doomed to fall over the precipice. Within the very systems of Earth lie keys to its regeneration—and ours. As we embark on the journey to Eloheh, we turn toward Mother Earth herself to learn lessons we will need to survive.

Stepping Back from the Precipice

One of the key characteristics of the natural world is adaptation, a concept the West has failed to apprehend. Indigenous peoples understand the importance of adaptation. As a result of our ability to adapt, no matter how extreme the conditions, Native people have been able to not just survive but thrive in every part of the world.

People who embrace the Western worldview, especially the version based on unjust power and unbridled capitalism, seek stabilization to maintain their wealth and power. This process of maintaining control through stabilization is called homeostasis. In a homeostatic system, no one rocks the boat. Again, this worldview is based on a false reality missing the point that change—sometimes big change—is inevitable. The current climate crisis, which wasn't inevitable, will require us to adapt.

Nature builds with different building blocks than do humans operating from a Western worldview. We have seen buildings ripped apart by a tornado next to a tree with a bird's nest still intact. We believe that Creator has given nature tools that we need to learn to use, such as unity and diversity, which are found throughout the landscape of creation. When building our homes and communities and cities, we would do well to explore the depths of practices such as biomimicry. Biomimicry refers to a set of practices in which humans learn from and mimic strategies of other species that have learned to survive and thrive. According to The Biomimicry Institute, it "is about valuing nature for what we can learn, not what we can extract, harvest, or domesticate. In the process, we learn about ourselves, our purpose, and our connection to each other and our home on Earth." We can learn from nature and even redesign our systems with the wisdom of nature in mind.

What most Americans view as stability is actually falling apart. Sometimes people refer to this process of natural degradation as entropy. Entropy is built into every system, whether human-made or natural. Things just naturally fall apart. We build a house, and over time it degrades and falls apart, being taken down by wind and rain, plants or mold or bugs. This is the way of nature. Nothing but the Earth lasts forever.

Conversely, from a Western worldview, people view the climate crisis as chaos. When rivers have what is considered a one-hundred-year flood three times in five years, it appears to many people to be chaos. When tornadoes slip out of their seasons and become a year-round threat, people call it chaos. The increase in frequency and severity of forest fires, droughts, and earthquakes, the worrisome rise in temperatures around the globe: all signal chaos to those operating out of the Western mind.

But Is This Chaos?

In reality—and this view can give us a measure of hope—the natural world is actually showing signs of adapting to the circumstances. Nature is stabilizing the Earth through adaptation. When circumstances occur that disrupt our natural systems, nature simply adapts. Nature is actually the great stabilizer; we are just looking at it in reverse.

Some of us are old enough to remember the margarine commercial where Mother Nature appears, and she is told to taste butter—which is actually margarine. Mother Nature then sends disaster on the people as she says, "It's not nice to fool Mother Nature." That silly commercial is partially correct: when we mess with the natural systems that run the planet, there can be severe consequences.

But it's not actually nature's wrath that we are experiencing; it's the natural world taking severe measures to stabilize the planet. The Western worldview has a fatal misunderstanding concerning both human preeminence and human permanence.

We realize that, for many of you reading this book, this is a new way of thinking, and we all learn through different stories and paradigms. If we could indulge those learning from a logical paradigm, we would like to explain what is happening in the most basic terms. A deeper dive into the natural transfer of the Earth's energy may help shed light on the problem.

It's All about Energy

Energy flows from the sun to the Earth in a long-term partnership. Besides plants, the number one transfer of energy on Earth is through microscopic sea creatures called phytoplankton. These little organisms supply one-third of the Earth's oxygen, without our impediment or intervention. So, we should be very grateful for these little critters. The number one consumer of phytoplankton are zooplankton, which are various small organisms we call plankton (what many whales eat). In other words: the greatest transfer of energy on Earth is taking place without most of us knowing or observing it.

As we move down the food chain, the secondary consumers are mostly fish and sea mammals such as whales. Way down the line of earthly and sea creatures that consume energy are what are called tertiary consumers, which include humans and other large land mammals. That we are tertiary consumers means this: in the large scheme of things, we are just nibblers. If you've ever seen goats graze, you know that they take a few bites here, a few bites there. In the whole scheme of things, in terms of consumption of energy, that's our rightful place on Earth: as nibblers.

Unfortunately, through creating so-called stable systems based on homogeneity (sameness), humans, in a relatively short time, have moved from tertiary consumers to *primary* consumers. Industrial farming, forest depletion, overfishing, mining for various minerals, drilling for petroleum products, contributing to disappearing wetlands, overconsumption of the Earth's water supply: these acts and more mean we are consuming energy far beyond the Earth's natural cycles and recharge rates. We as humans are creating imbalance and disharmony and taking a role that was never meant to be ours.

Fighting entropy is a losing battle. Attempting to fight nature will only have an unhappy result. Taking more than our share of the Earth's energy is bringing disastrous consequences to us all.

It appears that, for millennia, the whole of creation has been producing enough energy to allow humans limited consumption. But humanity, in just a few generations, has accelerated consumption exponentially. Mother Earth is now trying to rebalance the overuse through random "acts of nature." She is reclaiming her territory, spitting out the inhabitants, as Leviticus 18 frames it, to restore harmony. The top of the food chain is not us; it is Mother Earth herself.

As a result of human greed—fueled by empire and a faulty worldview—the Earth is being forced to consume the new primary consumer: namely, humanity. In order to restore the balance of energy to the rest of creation, the Earth has turned against the species (us) that has turned against her. This balance, or harmony, is the way Creator intended for the community of creation from the beginning and is the way nature works best.

What the West thinks of as ordered and stable is actually an ecosystem that is falling apart. Yet on the other hand, what might appear to humans with a Western worldview as nature's chaos is actually *stability* at this time. Earth continues to adapt, and that ability to adapt is constant. Mother Nature is relentless, and humanity is in a fight we cannot win.

In other words, when we view the world with the lens of Western dominance, we often miss entirely what is going on. Chaos can actually be order. Adaptation is stability.

Here are some important points to consider:

- The Creator created nature as open systems. These natural systems contain both unity and diversity as part of their nature.
- Homogenous, closed systems are built to die.
- Homogenous groups—such as groups sustained only by homogeneity of race, age, gender, or even monocultural hybrid/genetically modified crops—lead to eventual destruction.
- The nature of a closed system is to collapse in on itself or be consumed by other, more adaptive systems.
- The nature of open systems is to adapt.
- Real order is the reality of planning and perseverance in sustainable, open systems.
- Real order works *with* entropy, not against it, building open, adaptable systems of unity and diversity.
- Real chaos occurs when species attempt to fight entropy through unsustainable, closed, nonadaptive systems.
- Climate change is a result of the Western world's rejection of creation's natural laws, found in nature, and brings other disasters such as zoonosis (the transfer of animal disease to humans) that lead to worldwide pandemics and many chronic diseases.
- Nature adapts to allow the *most* species that cause the *least* harm to survive.

We know that this is a lot of sobering information to digest. (If you didn't believe us when we said in the introduction that this isn't your typical self-help book, maybe you do now!) Under the present circumstances, the final adaptation of nature might be human extinction. We only have a short time to come back from our own unsustainable chaos, back to nature's sustainable order. To do this, we need a change of mind and heart that comes with a change of worldview.

In an Indigenous worldview, we see all the systems of Earth—our food, our land, the health of the whole community of creation, economics, education, history, and politics—as connected. As we stated earlier, we call this way of being in harmony with everything around us by different words. In Cherokee, we call it Eloheh.

To help you understand the winding path many take toward living out Eloheh, we will now take you through brief accounts of our own more personal, Eloheh journeys, separately and then together. For even as we stand at a precipice as a species, we often come to the edge of survival as individuals. We want you to see us as people, like yourselves, who are on a journey.

Native Americans, descendants of settlers, and others: all of us find ourselves headed either toward well-being or away from it. We head toward a precipice or away from it. In different seasons of life, we may head different directions. The journey toward Eloheh means moving away from multiple precipices: as humans on a changing Earth, and as individuals longing for well-being.

We hope that, by hearing how we came to terms with the power of Indigenous values, you will deepen your own understandings and commitments. For you do not need to be Indigenous to embrace Indigenous values. You do, however, have to learn that Indigenous values grow out of Indigenous histories. The values we will talk about in this book are deeply rooted in communities and traditions and histories and shouldn't be simplistically extracted from them. We hope that, by hearing some Indigenous stories, you will learn more about the power Indigenous values hold for transformation, for hope, and for healing.

Our journeys begin long before we are born. We both come from some astonishing people. We wish we knew their stories better than we do, but we will share some of what we do know. We honor our ancestors by remembering them, by recalling what they contributed to the future they knew we would inherit and the values they wished to pass down.

3

PEOPLE

Edith's Journey

In the early 1800s, the Great Basin—which covers what we now call sections of Nevada, Idaho, Utah, Wyoming, California, and Oregon—was a kind of crossroads for groups of people, including mountain men, traders, trappers, and people of various Native tribes. This is why I (Edith) have such a rich history running through my veins. While some of my ancestors were Irish, Welsh, and French, most of my bloodlines stem from about eight Native American tribes, including Shoshone, Choctaw, Paiute, Crow, Piegan (Blackfoot: Piikáni), Mohawk, Umatilla, and Flathead.

My father's ancestry is particularly storied. One of my fifth great-grandfathers, Old Ignace LaMousse, was the leader of twenty-four Iroquois and Metis voyagers who came out west from the Kah-nawa':ke Mohawk reservation near Montreal, Quebec. Old Ignace traveled with a son, Young Ignace—Ignace Enos, as he was sometimes called. Young Ignace is my fourth great-grandfather.

Old Ignace's dream was to fulfill an old prophecy among the Plateau tribes. The prophecies, given in the eighteenth century by at least three men, Shining Shirt, Circling Raven, and Chief Illim-Spokanee, who all predicted that men in black robes—the Black Robes, as Jesuit missionaries would come to be called—would bring a special message from Creator (Great Mystery) to the people. It seems our Native people, who are very spiritual to begin with, were always interested in what others had to say about Creator.

Sadly, Old Ignace, who was killed by the Sioux, died trying to accomplish his dream. Instead, his son, Young Ignace, honored his father's death by completing the dream. Young Ignace was responsible for bringing the famous Jesuit missionary Pierre-Jean de Smet to the West. He had met de Smet at a Mandan village in what is now Council Bluffs, Iowa. The Black Robe de Smet became gravely ill on the journey, and Young Ignace nursed him back to health along the way.

Young Ignace married Mary Marie Washakie, my fourth great-grandmother, who was a sister to the great Shoshone Chief Washakie. Washakie was sometimes called the toughest warrior in the West. He and many of my relatives came from the clan or society known as the Shoshone White Knives. The White Knives (Tussawehee) were known as the bravest of the brave in protecting their people. Having grown up with many women from that lineage, I have no doubt that women such as Mary Marie were as tough as the men.

Mary Marie and her brother Chief Washakie's mother was called Lost Woman. Lost Woman married an Umatilla man named Passego, and they are my fifth great-grandparents. When he was a teenager, Paseego was rescued in a raid by Lost Woman's father from the Wasco Indian slave market at Celilo Falls. Paseego was also known as Crooked-Leg, because of an arrow that had been shot in his knee and prevented him from walking straight. Although he was Umatilla, he was raised by the Shoshone White Knives and became one of them. His rescuer, the Lost Woman's father, was a White Knives medicine man named Weasel Lungs. He was married to Blue Bird, and these were my sixth great-grandparents.

Mary Marie and Young Ignace had a son named John Enos, who became quite famous and even notorious, at least among settler people. John Enos is my third great-grandfather. He was called Enos because the Flathead people he was raised among as a child could not pronounce Ignace, so it came out as Enos. He was given the name John by de Smet himself. In John Enos's younger years, he guided the Bonneville expedition, a US military operation, across the South Pass, and later he guided the Fremont expedition, a purportedly scientific one. Unbeknownst to John Enos, both expeditions were looking for various routes that would become part of the Oregon Trail. The settlers had designs on the land, and the expeditions were crafted so that the United States could flood the area with settlers.

Of course, even though John Enos guided them, he never got the credit for it. Not a town or a county is named after him. Not a salt flat, nor a dam, nor even a big old awkward car is named after him. (At least the Ottawa Chief Pontiac got that.) Eventually, John Enos joined his White Knives relatives and was made a subchief in the Snake War, under Chief Has No Horse (a distant relative of mine, as is Sacajawea).

John Enos and his group of White Knives raided settlers and smuggled guns to the Rogue River Indians, keeping the flames of war stoked in southern Oregon. He is even said to have cut out the heart of Ben Wright, a particularly evil Indian agent stationed at Port Orford. Oregon had a bounty on his head, and vigilantes in one town even hung another Indian man they mistakenly thought was the notorious John Enos. But to the Shoshones and Paiutes, he was a patriot and freedom fighter.

John Enos married Julia LeBeouf, my third great-grandmother, a Blackfoot Piegan (Piikáni) woman. They had lots of children, who spread across the West.

On another branch of my paternal ancestry, my great-great-grandmother was captured by Curley, the young Crow Indian scout who reported the results of the Battle of the Little Bighorn to the army brass at Fort Robinson. Curly watched the battle at Little Bighorn take place from a tree in the distance. Curley, my great-great-grandfather, is buried in the cemetery at that site. My grandmother eventually left the Crows and returned to her Shoshone relatives. My Crow relatives say she was homesick; my Shoshone family says she escaped. But they both agree she swam the Powder River when it still had chunks of ice in it—while she was pregnant.

From that Crow-Shoshone line, my great-grandfather was born. He is a mystery; some say his name was Sam Idaho, but the genealogical trail has run cold on him. He was given the name Engavo (Enga-vooht), which means "Red Eyes," by the agent at Wind River. The Crow scout Curley became George Curley Old Elk, which later became the family surname. My Crow relatives still say Old Elk should be our name. But my grandfather, Jesse Harry, became an Engavo, as did my dad and all his children.

My great-uncle, Richard Engavo, was a wrangler for the Hole-in-the-Wall Gang, made famous by their time marauding with Butch Cassidy and the Sundance Kid. Most Shoshones are horse people, and Richard, especially, was a man of the horse. There was a stallion in the Old West that no one could break, called Midnight—no one except Richard Engavo, that is. A White guy was eventually given the credit for it, but one of my family members talked to an eyewitness to the event and found out the truth.

The Legacy of Boarding Schools

Touching the history of almost all Native American families in the United States and Canada is the residential boarding-school system. There were more than 350 such schools in the United States, funded by the government and most often run by churches. Modeled after the Carlisle Indian School in Pennsylvania, which was started by General Richard Henry Pratt and designed, as was said, to kill the Indian and save the child, the residential boarding-school system enacted harm, trauma, and abuse on generations of Indian children, including my dad's mom, Hazel Enos, who unfortunately attended Carlisle, was beaten chained up, and had pepper rubbed in her eyes.

Native parents were threatened with fines, the with-holding of food rations, and even imprisonment if they didn't allow their children to be taken to the schools. And while no one knows for sure how many Native children in the United States were affected, hundreds of thousands of children are estimated to have been taken from their parents and sent to residential schools between 1869 and the 1960s.

My father, Joe Engavo, was also one of them. An Eastern Shoshone tribal member born to Hazel (Enos) and Jesse Harry Engavo on May 19, 1929, my father was born on the Shoshone side of the Wind River Indian Reservation, in what we know as Wyoming. My dad was the oldest male of four children. In his preteen years, my father was sent to Flandreau, South Dakota, nine hundred miles from home. There he spent the most tumultuous and torturous years of his life in an Indian boarding school.

Before he left home, his grandmother had been teaching him to be the family medicine person and spiritual leader. Prior to being taken away to the residential school, my father's playground had been the rivers, fields, and mountains in our Rocky Mountain country. He knew places in the mountains where no White man had ever set foot. But agents of the federal government had told my grandparents that either he, as the oldest male, would attend boarding school or they would have to send all their children. My dad became the sacrifice.

When he returned from boarding school, my father was seventeen years old. Boarding school had left him bitter, lost between two worlds. His mother told him he needed to go to Sundance, a religious ceremony that lasts four days, to cleanse his mind, body, and spirit. Sundance is a renewal ceremony in which you stand and dance and suffer until you receive a vision or dream for your life direction. It is also meant to be an opportunity for sincere prayer for your family and for the people of your tribe and others.

Time passed quickly, and within just one year after my father returned home from the residential school, his mother died of cancer. Then, exactly one month after his mother died, his father died in a suspicious car crash.

That same year, my father got married and had a baby on the way. My dad and his wife, who was also a survivor of an Indian residential boarding school, were traumatized people. My father not only suffered the heinous crimes perpetrated against him in boarding school; on his return, he was left alone, with younger siblings to look after.

As the years went by, my dad and his wife dealt with their trauma by abusing alcohol. Heavy drinking and abusive behavior toward each other eventually led to a divorce, but only after they'd had seven children together.

My father's story is both singular and not singular. It is replicated over and over again among the survivors of Indian boarding schools. The harm was immense, and the intergenerational trauma is ongoing. Few Indigenous persons in the United States and Canada have been untouched by the legacy of Indian residential schools. Our government, hand in hand with churches, aimed to strip us of all the culture, language, religion, and community and family relationships we knew and loved. In so doing, they led us to a precipice that many of us are still trying to back away from.

Life on the Reservation

As time went on, my dad decided to leave our reservation and move to live among his Old Elk relatives in Crow Indian Country in Montana. Before he left the reservation, however, someone told him that he should go to a café in town to check out a beautiful young woman who was working there. My dad went up to the counter and ordered a chocolate milkshake. While a young woman was making it for him, he told her he was going to marry her.

She laughed it off. But three months later they were married. The young woman, Billie Daney, a Choctaw Indian, became his wife and then my mother. She was from Oklahoma, the fourth of five children of Edith and Ben Daney. She was raised in southeast Oklahoma in Choctaw

Country. Her father was a Southern Baptist minister who started many Choctaw churches in those Oklahoma hills. Her childhood was steeped in the life of the church. Unlike my dad, she had no crazy or outlandish life as a child. Her life was normal for the daughter of a poor family in that part of Oklahoma in the 1930s and 1940s. Mom went to a normal school and, as she says, had a plain and simple life. She grew up distant, however, from her Choctaw tribal traditions. I sometimes wonder how that disconnection affected her, and me, and our family as a whole.

Three years after my parents, Joe and Billie, were married, my brother Ben was born in 1965. A year later I was born, making me the youngest of my dad's nine children.

Growing up on the Wind River Indian Reservation was tough and sometimes traumatic. I grew up in a home that was, in a word, tumultuous. Between my siblings, cousins, and nieces and nephews, people were coming and going constantly. My first ten years were spent living in my grandmother's very small four-room log cabin. We burned a wood stove for heat, and we had a hand pump for water and an outhouse for a bathroom. We lived in that cabin until I was eleven years old, at which time my dad built another house next to my grandmother's house.

But I also remember great times. I knew my parents loved me and that they loved each other, and that was comforting. As kids growing up on a reservation in the Warm Valley just approaching the Rocky Mountains, we were free to dream and play and explore. I grew up with horses and cows, and a big—I mean a *very* big—backyard, with both a creek and a river running through it. During the spring we could not play in the river, because the runoff from the mountain snows would flood it, but the creek was the best at that time of year. We would go down to the creek and play in the mud and make a mud slide into the water. We would make up games and stay down at the creek for hours, until my mom would finally call us up to the house to eat or tell us to come in because it was getting dark.

On the weekends when my dad was home, he'd go fishing and I would tag along. Dad would have me find grasshoppers and dig worms for him, and then he and I would go down to the river. There he would show me how to bait a hook and wait patiently for a bite. I did not have much patience, however, and I would wander off and pick berries or play around the rocks and try to find horny toads to chase. Sometimes I wandered pretty far off from my dad, but he always seemed to know where I was. After he caught a fish or two, we would head back up to the house and he'd fry up some for lunch or dinner.

My dad had many horses, and we would ride all summer long. I would ride down to the general store, which was at least five miles away, sometimes by myself or with one of my sisters. We would tie the horses up on a hitching post when we went inside.

My dad was an announcer at the Pow Wow at Fort Washakie every summer for a few years. When the time came to get ready for the pow wow, my parents would start getting out the regalia, seeing what fit who and doing mending and adding to our regalia. At the start of the pow wow, we would always ride in on horseback in full regalia. My mom would warn us to watch for the whip lady, who would walk around the outside of the pow wow arena, keeping kids up to no good in line and out of trouble.

Summer was a time for fun but also for my dad and brothers to work with the cows. We all would go up to Crowheart, where my dad kept the cows at another grandpa's place. My mom would pack up a lunch for everyone, and we would all go up and bring the cows in and brand them and do the other tasks that needed to be done with them. Other times, we would all go up and do haying. That was a hard job for my dad and brothers. I would help my mom with the little kids, play in the waterways with my young nieces and nephews, and then just roam around and watch my dad and my brothers collect the hay.

My favorite horse was Mousy. I would ride Mousy around all summer, taking her to the best places to pick berries. I'd ride her to get away from things happening around the house or to be alone and just dream about a different life. Life was also hard growing up on the reservation, which I'll tell you about in a minute. But first: those berries.

One afternoon, when the chokecherries were in abundance, about six of us kids were excited. As we descended the hill toward the swimming hole at the river, we had noticed they were deep purple and ripe. That's the only time you want to eat chokecherries; otherwise they're bitter and inedible (hence the name). So, as we got to the berries, we all just started to pick. My brother Tom was with us, and he was in charge. Tom stood by and watched us as we began picking the berries and putting them in our butter bowls.

Tom watched us for a while, but then suddenly he yelled, "Stop!" We looked at him like he was crazy. He went on to tell us that we were being selfish by taking all the berries. "Pick some. Leave the rest," he told us.

I was baffled. That's why the berries were there: for us. Right? Tom went on to tell us that we should pick only from the middle of the bush, because we must share with all the other living critters in our area. He told us that the animals and birds had to eat, too, and that we had to share by only taking from the middle of the bush. The birds need to eat from the top so that they could carry the seeds to other places so that new berry plants could grow. And the small critters such as the snakes, squirrels, mice, and others needed to eat too. We did as we were told, and we were surprised to find out that, even when we only picked from the middle and left a lot of berries on the bushes, we still ended up with enough.

When we got home that afternoon, my brother took half the berries to freeze so we could make them into chokecherry gravy with fry bread in the winter. The rest of the berries we got to enjoy that day. My mom had cut a clean sheet into small squares, and she handed one to each of us. We poured the berries inside, added sugar, and folded the little square of cloth into a cone shape around the berries. We pressed the berries and sugar together until they created a kind of sauce, and then we sat around happily sucking out the juice from the cloth. After we had sucked out all the sweet juice, we would eat the mushy berries. I guess this was like the kind of trip wealthier kids had when their parents took them to the Dairy Queen.

In any case, the lesson that my brother Tom was trying to teach us that day did not really sink in until Randy and I had grandchildren. One day I was out picking berries with our first grandson, and I suddenly remembered what my brother had said to me so many years ago.

So now that's how I pick berries and how I teach our grandchildren to pick them. I tell them the words my brother told us that one summer day: pick some, leave the rest.

Disturbing Times

My dad drank a lot, as an attempt to cope with the trauma of his boarding-school experience and losing his parents at such an early age. At one point, my mom left him because he got ready to hit her. She told him if he did, that would be the last time he would ever see her. He never hit my mom, but he did keep drinking, and she left him for over a year. With five of the youngest kids—including me, my brother, and three of my half-siblings—Mom went to Oklahoma for over a year. My mom started a job and put the oldest kids into school, and we lived with my grandparents until my dad stopped drinking.

He did stop, for a bit. He came and got my mom, me, my brothers, and my sister, and we went back to Wyoming. Dad went back to drinking, though, for a short while after that. I don't know what made him stop for good, but eventually he did. I was about eleven years old when he stopped drinking, which was also about the time we moved into the new house he built.

I had to grow up faster than any child should, and I saw and experienced things that no kid should. At the age of twelve, I was sexually abused by one of my half brothers. That abuse lasted for several years. It went on until he left home. He told me to keep it a secret and that if I did tell, no one would believe me anyway. As a child, I thought that was true.

When this same half brother tried to abuse a friend of mine, she and I went to my mother to tell her what had happened. We told my mom what that brother had tried to do to my friend. My mother responded that it couldn't be true, that he would never do that.

That day, I realized I could never tell my parents about any of the abuse that had happened to me. I stuffed it down and kept to myself, mostly in my room. I was the quiet child who never got into trouble. My parents had their hands full with the rest of the children and all the trouble they were making, so I kind of faded into the background of their attention.

I didn't have many friends in school. Although I seemed like a loner who didn't want to spend time with people, I wanted friends. I longed for them. I guess the first real friend I had was in the third grade. We would play together at recess and sit next to each other in class, and I would go over to her house and play. She was my friend until one day at recess, when a bully came up to us and started to hit us. The girl told me to hit my friend, and I said no. But she kept hitting me and hitting me some more. So, to make her stop, I hit my friend, and she started to cry. The bully was happy and walked away, but my friend said she hated me. She and her family soon moved into town, and I didn't see her again until high school. Even then she would not talk to me.

Between the abuse and incidents like that, I became a very lonely child, keeping to myself. I put my nose in books and dreamed of a better life. I just did not know what to do with all my feelings about the trauma I had endured. I had very low self-esteem. I didn't like the color of my skin, the color of my hair, how poor we were, or the hand-me-downs from my older sisters I had to wear. I would daydream that we were a family like the Brady Bunch, where everything was always OK by the end of the episode.

But of course, in real life, it was never that simple.

Toward the Edge

I was introduced to drugs and alcohol at an early age. Those substances seemed to take away a lot of pain that I was feeling. In 1984, I barely graduated from high school. I thought I wanted to go into the Air Force with a friend of mine, but my parents talked me into going to college off the reservation instead.

Bacone Indian College was in southeast Oklahoma, near my mother's family. But I did not know that side of my family very well, so I felt like a stranger in a strange land. My new situation at college totally scared me, and right after I got to campus, I called my parents, crying and begging to come back home to Wyoming. But my mom would not allow it. She would not even let me talk to my dad, because she knew he would give in to me. By the end of that first week, I was already in trouble with the dean of students because we had a party in one of the dorm rooms. That was my first week of college.

I made a few friends and went to a lot of parties full of drugs and alcohol. Strangely, I always made it to church on Sundays, simply because that's the routine with which I had grown up. My mom wanted her children to be exposed to the church. On the reservation, when I was younger, a pastor and his wife showed me an angry God who judged every action I took. If I did not stay in line, their God would send me to hell. That God would not love me. Because I thought I was a bad person, that started a cycle: every time I would mess up, get drunk, or get high, I would say the "sinner's prayer." Wash, rinse, repeat. I don't know how many times I said the sinner's prayer while still high or hungover from the night before. But I always went to church on Sunday mornings, on campus, because I knew that's what my mom would want me to do.

Eventually I started going to another church full of White people. It was OK at first, and I felt love and care from the people there. But at the same time, I just did not fit in. I was embarrassed by my skin color and where I came from. Looking back, I'm sure that having gone through sexual abuse and other childhood traumas contributed much to my low sense of self-worth.

I had met a Mowa Choctaw girl from southern Alabama in one of my classes, and we became roommates. We did all sorts of fun things together, such as going to movies. We would also get high and drunk together, and often we would end up at parties. Although I had made a friend, this lifestyle left me feeling empty.

With Christmas just around the corner, I was at perhaps the worst point in my life. I couldn't face going home and encountering my parents, who had high hopes that I might be able to make it off the reservation. I just couldn't stomach the idea of letting my parents down. I imagined their disappointment, their sadness at what I had become. After all they had been through—residential schooling, alcoholism, racism, poverty, prejudice, parenting my siblings—I didn't want them to see who I had become, so I tried taking my life by slitting my wrists. I was hauled from school in an ambulance to the emergency room and then kept there for observation.

I ended up in treatment in Springfield, Missouri, and then for two years in Garrison, New York, all through a program called Teen Challenge. The program was a church-based treatment center. There I was again, being introduced to another kind of Christianity. And there I was again, feeling like I did not fit in. I tried so hard, but I still felt like I was inadequate for Creator's love.

I finished the program after two years of constantly fighting with Creator. I went back to Oklahoma and enrolled in Bacone's school for radiology. I found I was passionate about that field, and I decided that was what I wanted to do with my life.

About that time, I decided to tell the truth about the sexual abuse from my half brother, so I reached out to an uncle on my mother's side whom I was close to. I told him what had happened to me. He told me that we all have skeletons in our closets and that's where they need to stay. That was the end of the conversation.

That's not great advice for a survivor of sexual abuse, someone still hurting as much as I was. I was in shock. My uncle never brought it up again. I decided to go talk to his sister, my auntie. When I told her the story of the yearslong abuse I had experienced, she basically said the same thing my uncle had. Her rationale was, "Why would he [my half brother] do that to you when he knows better?" She finally said, "He would never do that to you." In other words, she blamed me and suggested I was making it all up.

When I was at the Teen Challenge's Walter Hoving Home in New York, I talked about this trauma with my counselor on multiple occasions. At one point, she told me, "Well, you just have to pray, and God will forgive you for that sin."

On all three occasions that I told people about the abuse I had endured, either I was not believed, I was told that it was somehow my fault, or I was told not to talk about it (sometimes multiple of these messages at once). So I didn't. I told myself I would never say anything again about the sexual trauma I experienced. The pain and betrayal remained deep in my spirit.

I was living much like my father had when he returned from boarding school. When we are living between two worlds, we hold the trauma we have experienced inside. We find strategies we think will help us survive, but they end up harming us.

This is what they call intergenerational trauma. It's like hopping on a bike and trying to ride away from all the pain. But after a while, you see that the bike is just stationary. No matter how hard you pedal, you end up at the same place you started. You thought you were moving away from the trauma, but you realize you are staying in the same place.

You're still on the precipice. And it's still a long way down.

4

IDENTITY

Randy's Journey

Just eking out a living can take everything you've got.

My (Randy's) mom's dad was a coal miner who died early in life, though we are uncertain as to the cause. His dad was also a coal miner, who died in a coal mining accident. The grandfather I knew, my mother's stepfather, was a coal miner who died of black lung disease from the mines. All my mom's brothers and half brothers were coal miners at some point in their lives. I am of the first generation on my mother's side not destined to work the mines.

Mom was born in 1927. In north-central Alabama, where my mother grew up, coal miners had it rough. My mom's father, Edward Lee Broadhead, was a coal miner and a skilled musician. They say he played anything with strings well, but the mandolin was his favorite. Almost everything I ever heard about my grandpa Broadhead was from my maternal grandmother. Later I had to discover his family history, and much of the story of our maternal Cherokee roots, on my own.

Prior to marrying my grandfather, Edward, Grandma, whose name was Nettie, had been a widow without children, having lost her only child to spinal meningitis. Then her second husband, my grandfather, died after they had three children together. At the time, my mother was only two years old. Life was already tough for Grandma when my grandpa died, and she found herself now surviving a second husband. Nettie was a kind and very strong woman and did her best to keep her family clothed and fed. Grandma was a widow three times before she herself went to her grave.

Before he died, Edward had asked his good friend, widower Sam Love, to take care of his wife and children. So, after Grandpa Broadhead died, Grandma married Sam Love.

My grandpa Love was a drinker in his early years, as was my grandpa Broadhead, to a degree. *Alcoholic* is a term that probably would have fit both, although it wasn't used much in the twenties and thirties. They brewed their own moonshine back then. The two men had worked hard together as miners. They'd succeeded in bringing the United Mine Workers union to Blount County, Alabama, and they paid for that right every day by keeping the coal coming out of those mines in the mountains of rural Alabama.

My mother and her two older brothers were raised in a coal camp built by Lehigh Coal. She said they rarely saw meat on the table when she was young. The only way they stayed healthy at all in those days was by eating the vegetables they grew and an occasional possum or squirrel. She tells of times when a sweet potato was an entire meal. Mom got her first pair of new shoes when she was thirteen. She didn't wear them to school, though, because the school was so far away, and the long walks would have worn them out too quickly.

My mom had two older brothers, but she was the oldest daughter, and that practically meant being a mom herself to her six younger half brothers and sisters. While they were growing up, Grandma would often be working out in the fields chopping cotton. My mother, if she wasn't working with her mother, would be at home, standing on a crate to reach the stove and preparing meals for the whole family.

My dad had it a little better than Mom did, but not by much, growing up in rural Mississippi with eight brothers and sisters. The Woodleys were farmers. My grandpa Woodley raised the best yellow-meated watermelons I have ever had. Grandma Woodley was a feisty little woman—the queen bee of her house—and she kept her kitchen fit for some of the best southern cooking around. Though she was diabetic, I have found that her coconut cakes and banana pudding are unequaled to this day.

After the bombing of Pearl Harbor, Dad set his sights on doing his patriotic duty, so he joined the Navy the day after he graduated from Burnsville High School. To keep his mother from worrying, he wrote home every week for the entire three years. He spent most of his time in the South Pacific. After World War II, my dad ended up in Birmingham, Alabama, at his older sister's home. Dad had gotten a job in Birmingham as a mover for Sears Roebuck. Though always charming and flirtatious, he was also a grown man home from war, and it was time to start thinking about a family.

My parents met at the Sears store in Birmingham, where my mother worked at the candy counter. She had had to quit her schooling in her early teens and move to the city to work, as was often the obligation of the older children in poor families. Mom was seventeen now, living with an aunt and sending money back home to her parents. The story goes that the first time they met, my dad tried to startle her by saying "Boo!" "Boo, yourself," she replied calmly. He kept trying to win her attention and affection, but she was not about to go out with a former sailor.

Dad's pursuits got him nowhere until one day when he hurt his back in an elevator accident at Sears, not far from the candy counter where my mother worked. As the medics were carrying him away on a stretcher, Mom relented. She walked over to the stretcher and said, "All right, I'll go out with you." In a few short months, they were married. I was their fourth and final child. Their marriage lasted just a few weeks short of seventy-five years. They passed away in the summer of 2021 within weeks of each other.

Our family moved around Alabama a few times and even to Michigan for a short stint. Eventually, I was born in Andalusia, Alabama, in the early morning hours of July 27, 1956—even though I wasn't supposed to be. Three different doctors had encouraged my mother to abort me for her health, but my mother was not convinced by their reasoning. Anne Woodley was not well educated in the formal sense, but she was wise and intuitive. She believed in the value of her own child coming into the world; for that, I am grateful.

Though Dad was running a restaurant and selling insurance, there was never enough money to get ahead. Alabama economics still did not allow them to make ends meet. Mom worked at the Chicken Shack restaurant they bought and took in ironing at three dollars a basket. Those baskets were always, as she said, "piled high." Between caring for me and my three siblings and working part-time at the restaurant, she didn't have enough hours in a day. Mom needed nearly all day just to iron one basket of laundry.

When I was only six months old, we moved to Ypsilanti, Michigan, just southeast of Detroit. Dad had a brother there who was doing well for himself in a branch of the auto industry. My parents were glad for the opportunity to make a better life for themselves and for us kids.

Dad worked for Ford Motor Company for a short time, and eventually he was able to start his own auto-upholstery business, which he ran successfully for the next seventeen years. Detroit was somewhat of a mecca for Southerners of all colors in those days. As my dad used to say, "In the South they taught us the three R's: readin', writin' and the road to Detroit."

After World War II, the old B-24 bomber plants were all turned into automobile factories, and the automakers were putting out cars as fast as they could. Communities such as Willow Run, where we lived, existed almost solely because of automobiles. Most of the people in Willow Run had migrated from the South, from conditions similar to those of my own family. Whether you came from a West Virginia, Kentucky, or Alabama coal mine, it was the same old poor. For many poor families, the pay, hours, and working conditions at the automobile factories made the move worth leaving home. And the unions up north were strong, so there was job security.

I grew up hearing the word *home* quite often. My parents used it when they referred to their relatives who were still down in Alabama and Mississippi—although at one time or another, it seems like most of my mom's relatives lived with us. My parents were delighted to join any conversation that began with the phrase, "Did you hear what happened back home?" Home to them was down South. It took them many years to return there. Their friends were largely other people from the South, who in essence could have been relatives—people who fit right in with our own manners and customs.

At about nine years old, I was sitting around with my family at a Friday night gathering in a church member's home. At least half of the members of our Baptist church in Michigan had Cherokee, Choctaw, Creek, or Shawnee roots. Every one of them was proud of that fact. That evening they were playing guitars and swapping stories of the old days. Several told about how their grandparents spoke their Native American language, but no one there seemed to have a current connection to their Indigenous roots.

That seemed wrong to me. Why have such a proud heritage and be disconnected from it? I knew my family had Indigenous roots, and I decided right then that was not the kind of Indian I wanted to be. I began to read Native American books exclusively and seek out Native American friends.

I became intrigued by these ideas of home, identity, belonging, community, and family. I got curious about how we decide who we are and what origin story we craft for ourselves. Where did we come from, and what stories create our identities? What families do we claim, and which families claim us? In those days, I watched as people who were living far away from homemade family wherever they went. I became eager to learn about my own ancestry, the legacies and lines that made me who I was.

What Makes an Indian?

None of us just appeared in this world without a context. We are who we are, proud or ashamed or both, because of our ancestors. I am an amalgamation of mostly European peoples such as English, Scottish, Irish, Bavarian German, French, Danish, Swedish, and a little Portuguese, along with a little Ethiopian, Ashkenazi Jew, and a smidgen of Cherokee Indian. My identity as a Cherokee descendant is recorded by the United Keetoowah Band tribal membership committee as three-sixteenths Cherokee. The day I received my letter recognizing my legal descendance was one of the proudest days of my life.

On one hand, that three-sixteenths blood quantum represents, as my mother-in-law used to say, "just a thimble full." On the other hand, as I began to form my identity, ignoring this significant part of who I was would have seemed reckless when it was so dear to me.

Over the years, I have forged deep connections with Indigenous communities in North America and all over the world, which I'll talk about later in the book. This odd and wonderful mixture of peoples is the way Great Mystery made me, and that's OK with me, as I have a rich heritage. Although Woodley is an English surname, long ago I accepted my Cherokee (Keetoowah) identity as primary. This identity formation happened sometime around the age of nine, which was the time I became interested in these questions. Over the years, I have wrestled with my identity as a mixed blood, which will come up again later in the book. But in short, thinking of myself primarily as Keetoowah does not diminish my other bloodlines and relatives; rather, I think it enhances them.

On my mom's side I descend from both Oliver Cromwell, who was a Protestant political zealot, and George Calvert, High Lord Baltimore, who established the Catholic sanctuary of Maryland. Isn't that ironic? Having been presented, along with Edith, the 2021 Ecumenist of the

Year Award from the Ecumenical Ministries of Oregon, I'd like to think I may have helped mend some of that rift.

My Native ancestry comes from both of my parents. On one line of my mother's side, we are descended from Chief Gu-le-quah (translated from Cherokee as Big Acorn), a Chickamaugan leader who was cited as one of the forty-two chiefs and leading men of that Cherokee group fighting against the United States at the time. He signed the Treaty of Holston in 1791 and later became a Cherokee Old Settler, which in Cherokee history links him and my loyalties to the Keetoowah Band. Cherokee ancestry on my dad's side appears as well through several lines.

The ancient Woodleys were likely Danish Vikings who traveled in the ninth century with King Rollen to invade Paris. Settling in Normandy for a while, their descendants then invaded England in 1066 with William the Conqueror. They spent over five hundred years in Devonshire, England, during which time the name was recorded as "those living in the lea (meadow) in the woods." The Woodleys, true to their Viking heritage, sailed ships back and forth from England to Jamestown and finally settled in that colony in the 1630s. Most of my father's (and mother's) European lines are early American settlers, with a few eventually, through marriage and other circumstances, connected to Cherokees.

I'm thankful to all my ancestors. I'm guessing that, on the other side of this life, they are not separated by ethnicity or race or genealogy. I doubt they are fighting each other over my identity or theirs.

Childhood Turmoil

As my family adjusted to life in Michigan, tensions of all kinds threaded themselves through my daily life. The community of Willow Run was where I became a city boy. I faced the stress of growing up in a place no one wanted to call home. To make matters worse, we lived in eight different houses before I graduated from high school. I felt dissatisfied with much of urban life. My soul cried out for the deep country setting of my relatives in Alabama, Mississippi, and Oklahoma, whom we often visited.

I also felt the anxiety of being a mixed-blood Cherokee—which I was proud of but which no one else wanted to talk about as being relevant to our current identity. There was also the hurt of not getting the time and attention I wanted from hardworking parents—especially from my father. By the time I was twelve years old, those tensions had twisted me for long enough that they began to explode.

I attended school in a low-income, diverse district. There was enough hurt all around us to keep anyone who chose to be angry and violent without reason. People carried guns and knives to school just as a matter of course. At twelve I was already carrying a Slim Jim knife with a seven-inch blade in my pocket, and I figured if that failed, I could use the backup straight razor in my shoe. I was skipping school, constantly getting into fights, and being suspended for one reason or another, and I had accrued a record with the juvenile court system.

My parents wanted me to find positive friends, but I was unwilling to risk trying to have friendship with the good kids. Eventually, I found plenty of others who felt as bad about themselves as I did. The bad kids had been rejected enough times that they no longer cared. By hanging out with them, I at least found some form of acceptance. But it wasn't without a price.

By seventh grade, I was skipping school often. My friends and I would meet under the viaduct where the hoboes hung out, and we'd drink wine. It was a battle just to survive without getting beat up. At school, no one went into the dreaded bathroom alone, and getting safely home from school was always an adventure. Pornography was passed around like candy, and many guys in the junior high already claimed more sexual exploits than humanly possible. It was the late sixties. I loved to dance, and at all the parties in our town, Motown music was the standard.

While our parents were trying to get ahead through hard work—which not only put bread on the table but earned them respect—the children of Willow Run were learning to gain notoriety through sex, alcohol, fighting, and how well we could dance at parties. These were the rites of passage of my teen years.

The one other activity that could grant you instant fame in our community was athletic ability. The guys who excelled in sports were the princes of the town. I had gotten a slow start in this area, largely because my dad spent a lot of time working and didn't have time to teach me anything related to sports. He was working hard to keep his business running. My brother, nine years older than I was, was busy dating and preparing for college. It's hard to imagine, if you know me now, but I was a skinny kid. Perhaps *gangly* would be a better description: gangly and terribly uncoordinated. I needed help in developing athletic skills, lest I lose out completely. When a kid lost out in sports in my community, he was marked for life. Fortunately, my sister was a cheerleader who married an athletic star, and my brother-in-law took an interest in helping me. Over time, I began to show a little athletic prowess.

Before my seventh grade year was over, my parents had decided to move away from Willow Run. I hated the idea of moving, but I also knew that my troubles were one of the main reasons they decided to leave. By this time, I had been both arrested for truancy as a juvenile and charged with destruction of property. The vice principal had assured my father that if I got into any more fights at school, I would be not just suspended but expelled for the remainder of the year. From my point of view, I was building my reputation up very well. And now they wanted me to leave? I hated it, and some of that spewed over in to how I treated my parents, especially my dad.

Saline, Michigan, is only twenty miles from Ypsilanti, but the two towns were worlds apart. Saline was an old German farming community, and the population was almost all White. My first day in the eighth grade at Saline, I did what I normally would do: I cut class. I began walking the three miles back to the new home my dad had built for us out in the country. By this time, I had lost one of my weapons and I carried only the straight razor in my shoe. As I was walking down the country road, I saw a car slowing down. Thinking it was the truancy officer and that I would be arrested and searched, I quickly dug out the straight razor from my shoe and threw it in the nearby cornfield. It only turned out to be a man looking for an address.

I can see now that the incident was somehow a turning point for me. I began to realize that trouble was not actually looking for me in that small farm town. I had to try to learn how not to be a gangster. But it wouldn't be easy.

There I was in eighth grade at Saline Junior High, where I had become an instant novelty. I had grown up in a mostly culturally Black environment, with some White, Latinx, and Asian friends, and a few Indians. My clothes were very different from the clothes of the average farmer's son in Saline. My walk placed me as obviously from somewhere near Detroit. And when I hit the dance floor, they knew Saline had been invaded by another culture, though many could not quite figure out what this strange mixture was about. Here I was, a White-presenting young man who thought of himself as an Indian but spoke Ebonics, as it was known back then.

Because I was so different and had prior experience with alcohol and dating, I repelled the establishment, impressed my classmates, and drew the attention of some of the older students—at first to put me in my place but later to become one of them. At fourteen, I was crossing the border north into Canada and south into Ohio, where the drinking age was eighteen, using a fake ID and getting drunk with the older guys. The parties, the sexual conquests, the alcohol, and finally the drugs were all becoming almost second nature to me. I also began playing music, starting out on the bass guitar. Eventually I ended up in a rock band.

As a teenager, I really thought that I had everything a young man could want. Strange, now, to reflect on how I even thought I had an advanced philosophical perspective. I was a fan of Martin Luther King Jr. and the American Indian Movement, and I subscribed to several underground newspapers, including the *Akwesasne Notes*. I was in full bloom in the folly of my youth.

My best friend was Dave Johnson. We had both been chosen to hang out with the older guys. What more could we ask for? Dave and I had the girls, a reputation as nice but tough guys, the drugs and alcohol, the sports achievements, and the popularity that some kids would have died for. Yet in the still of the night, we would admit to each other a sense of emptiness. We knew that we were missing something deep in our souls, even though we didn't have words for it.

In the eighth grade, I figured out that I was much faster than most of the kids at school. Though raw in every sense of the word, and undisciplined, I was fast. Track became one positive influence in my life. As a freshman, I earned my varsity letter after only two meets; I was told I was the first freshman at Saline High to ever to achieve this feat. But that success was short lived because of my outside activities. In my freshman year, I was charged with breaking and entering an elementary school to steal lunch tickets and sell them. After being suspended from school, I was expelled from the track team, which cost me my varsity letter.

Even during these early delinquent years, I had a quiet, more private side. Some of my new farm-kid friends had taught me to hunt. I had grown up fishing on my grandfather's pond in Mississippi and snagging redhorse in the river, which my uncles in Alabama taught me to do while on summer vacations. After school and on Saturdays, I would often wander off alone in the woods, sometimes hunting or fishing but often just being in nature. Those times alone in the woods became my solace, giving me peace in ways that satisfied my whole being. I'd spend hours just lying down on the ground with the sun on my face, listening to the creek run, and observing nature's activity around me. Somehow, I did not feel so alone when I was watching the birds, squirrels, deer, and rabbits. It was as if I were praying without making any words. And somehow, somewhere, I knew Creator was answering my prayers.

Teenage Angst

I spent a lot of time running away my freshman year in high school. There were many nights spent arguing with my parents about my rights. I guess I was angry at my father for working so much and ignoring me. I know a big part of it also was just feeling like I never fit in, no matter how cool I looked from the outside. Also, it was just the times. That was the summer I first tried marijuana. After that first drug incident, it was just one new drug after the next. This new pastime, along with the rock band, opened me up to a whole new world of friends.

I had crossed over into another subculture: the freaks, sometimes called hippies. With this new society came new parties, outdoor concerts, new sex partners, and lots of rock 'n' roll. But accompanying all the new experiences was a slowly increasing feeling of weariness and frustration.

During this time, I made another huge mistake. I had been running indoor track during the winter and outdoor track during the spring. In almost every event I participated, I set records. Running gave me a sense of freedom. Track and field required no expensive accoutrements: just shoes, socks, a jockstrap, shorts, and a shirt. There was nothing on those few lanes except me and the other guys. With a combination of raw strength and courage, I was good—really good. Somehow that feeling of pride in my running began to transfer into the essence of my being. My one great talent was the thing that gave me a sense of worth. In track I was a winner, not just because I almost always won but because it was just me and my speed, nothing else. In track, I felt like a warrior.

The years 1972 and 1973 were important for Native people, especially young people. First, there was the Trail of Broken Treaties when Native Americans, led by the American Indian Movement, traveled across the country in protest of the US government's failure to honor treaties they entered with Native American nations. When they arrived in Washington, DC, they took over the Department of the Interior's Bureau of Indian Affairs building and occupied it in protest. Afterward, many ended up on the Pine Ridge Reservation in South Dakota, where they occupied a church at the old Wounded Knee massacre site.

During the 1973 siege at Wounded Knee, I began wearing my hair in braids and sporting a hawk feather occasionally. That same year, when I reported for the new indoor track season with my new look, it did not sit well with the coach. Of course, I'm sure the track coach had also heard all the rumors of my drug use, and my bad attitude was all too evident. He ordered me off the team for a week and told me to come back with a new look and a new attitude.

As you might guess, I did not respond well to his condemnation. But I blamed it all on his reaction to my regalia, reasoning he was just another White racist. Although I had placed well in the state track meet and had college scouts coming to practice to watch me run, I chose not to come back to track after that week.

In my young mind, I was identifying with five hundred years of oppression, with the people at Wounded Knee, with the Mohawks on the Canada–New York border, and other Indigenous people who had been wronged in so many ways throughout history. I was grasping for my identity. Not returning to compete in track and field was only one of the many foolish decisions I made over the next few years.

College Dropout

Somehow I got into Eastern Michigan University in a program for troubled students. I isolated myself from my roommates during the first days of college. I arrived early and plastered my side of the room with Indian posters and radical Native sayings. That first day I overheard someone say to my roommate, "Has anyone met the chief yet?" They both laughed. I decided from that point on I would reject them as racists. By the end of October, I had no friends at college, was failing most classes, and was both emotionally and spiritually empty.

By midsemester, I had dropped out, and my life became seemingly one endless downhill spiral. More drugs, more sex partners, more booze—more than any young man could afford. I had entered college mainly to find a bigger market for the drugs I was dealing. The catch was that they had taken their toll on my brain, to the point where I could hardly finish a sentence without losing my train of thought or wondering what I had just said.

After leaving college, I had no direction. The next year was one of the worst years of my life. Between a drug overdose, an addiction problem, a traumatic relationship breakup, and the deaths of several people close to me, I began to see the proverbial handwriting on the wall.

I wasn't sure how to walk myself back from the precipice of despair, addiction, and loneliness, but I knew I couldn't keep going the direction I was going. I remember eavesdropping on a conversation between my parents and my older sister. They all seemed to agree that I was headed either to prison or to the grave.

What they didn't realize was that I was ready to do just about anything to find the Harmony Way. I didn't yet know what that would be or who would help me. But I intuited, even then, that the journey to Eloheh would involve returning to myself—to my truest self—and to the Indigenous worldview buried within my ancestral story.

PART II

FINDING A NEW MAP

5

SWEAT LODGES

Questioning Religion, Seeking Spirituality

A Kiowa man in his late seventies once told us one of the most poignant stories about Indian boarding schools we've ever heard. When he was eight years old, a White missionary had come to his parents' home in the country. The missionary basically guilted his parents and several other parents in the community into sending him and a few other boys to the Riverside Indian Boarding School in Anadarko, Oklahoma.

The boys arrived in their best clothes, with hair in nice long braids and their finest regalia. The missionary—again, working in conjunction with the federal government—had made this place sound very special, so the families had wanted their sons to appear in their very best. An unwelcome surprise awaited them at the school.

First, the boys were stripped of all their clothes and given uniforms. School staff threw their clothes away, put the kids through a delousing treatment, put bowls on their heads, and cut off their long hair. The teachers told them the boys needed to have short hair to become civilized and to be made acceptable to God. In Kiowa culture, as in most Indian cultures, to cut one's hair was a sign of grieving. Then they were marched off to their new living quarters and sent to bed. The Kiowa elder remembers crying himself to sleep that night.

The next day was Sunday. The teachers marched them to the chapel and showed each, in turn, a picture of Jesus. They told the boys that Jesus, God's own son, loved them. This seemed very strange to the boys, and they discussed it among themselves later. Here they had been stripped of the dignity of their hair to be accepted by God, but God's own son had long hair.

I (Randy) thought of this story recently as I reflected on the two years that I spent as a missionary in Alaska. Everyone who knew me as a young man was surprised that I ended up as a missionary—and I was too. But like so many young people in my generation, desperate after a long struggle, I had eventually turned to religion. After I graduated from college, I looked for something spiritual to fill a void in my soul. During the late 1960s and early 1970s, some young people turned to Buddhism, others to Hare Krishna. But because of my parents' influence early on in life, I had turned to Jesus. I straightened out my life, started going to church, went back to college, and eventually answered what Christians refer to as a call to ministry.

I was married at the time to someone else, and we had a beautiful young daughter, Leanna. We became missionaries and began working at a school for Alaskan Native youth. We were called "teaching parents," working within a behavioral-modification system that housed around ten Native youth.

This situation turned out to be oddly, uncomfortably, and eerily familiar. We were to befriend the youth, yes. But we were also in a position of controlling and disciplining them. Even if we didn't intend to do so, we were part of severing their ties to culture and family and bringing them into conformity with a Western worldview.

During those two years, I often felt as though I was on the verge of a nervous breakdown. The tension—between the two worlds in which I was living, between the expectations placed on me and my identification with the young people in our care—resulted in mental anguish. My health began to deteriorate. I came to understand that something like this might be what my own Cherokee ancestors went through. History was repeating itself.

I deeply regret the negative impact we had on the lives of the Native youth there. Even during those years, I tried to make amends. I tried to work both in the system and around it. I must have gained some trust, because several of the Native youth kept in touch over the years. But since then, whenever opportunities like this—to work in systems that exercise such control over other human beings—have arisen, I have rejected them outright.

As I look back on this experience, I can find only a little bit of good in it: that is, that I learned to identify the feelings that perpetrators of control over individuals experience. I can now imagine, to a small degree, the anguish of the patrons and matrons at the Indian boarding schools who were Native American. At least I hope they were conflicted. Because not all the staff at these schools were descendants of settlers, the schools sometimes employed Native people. They had to make sure the children were dressed in their itchy wool uniforms and answered to a number rather than a name. They had to enforce the regimented, military-like lifestyle for children from their own communities. They were being called on to perpetrate the same atrocities on others that they themselves had likely suffered.

In no way should this point minimize the pain of the victims of cultural atrocities, nor excuse those who participated in mentally, emotionally, physically, or sexually abusing innocent children. But my time at the Alaskan school gave me at least a slight understanding of the temptation to dehumanize another individual, even someone from my own culture, a sense of what it is to flaunt a "superior religion." Today I can easily recognize the widespread cultural guilt and shame—and denial—in which so many Americans live, because they have never dealt with this history.

Well-being, as individuals and groups, depends on an honest reckoning with the past. You can't build a future of wholeness and harmony without naming past harm you've done and that has been done to you. As we journey toward Eloheh, we don't only look forward, toward the values we want to embody and the people we want to be. We look backward, too, to make sense of the values that have shaped us and the people we have been. This is all part of the decolonizing process.

Learning from the Past

I left Alaska determined never to oppress anyone, especially Native Americans, again. I went to seminary after our return from Alaska, and while there, I studied American church history. I spent hundreds and perhaps thousands of hours in original research concerning the mission history of my own Cherokee ancestors. I was on my own journey toward understanding Indigenous values. Indigenous values are connected to Indigenous history, and you can't learn one without learning the other. And Indigenous history includes contact with missionaries and settlers.

Early on, my studies led me to the journals of two Baptist missionaries, Evan and John Jones. Since my time in Alaska, I had felt the weight of being a missionary oppressor, and I longed to learn more about the history of missions. Although Evan and John Jones held worldviews limited by their era, they also managed to reinforce Cherokee people's dignity rather than diminish it. They were also staunch abolitionists. Along with Cherokee coworker Rev. Jesse Bushyhead, the Joneses trained dozens of Cherokee pastors, many of whom went on to become Cherokee national leaders.

Other accomplishments resulted in a Cherokee New Testament, an all–Cherokee language Native discipling and training school, the revival of many Cherokee traditional religious beliefs and principles—which other missionaries had tried to expunge—and a Cherokee printing press and newspaper.

Jesse Bushyhead and the Joneses left an impression in my heart and mind forever. Reading their original letters and journals helped me gain hope at the time, helped me learn how not to use religion as a tool for oppressing people again.

Another reality struck hard and deep just before I began my senior year of seminary. My spouse decided to end our seven years of marriage, leaving me as a single father to my six-year-old daughter. I was devastated. Without the constant help and encouragement from professors and friends, I would not have made it. Anger, rejection, self-doubt, jealousy, betrayal: I felt them all, in their rawest forms. Finally, after about six months, I accepted her decision. I found that even when I was at the bottom, in my darkest hour, Creator was still there.

One of the ways Creator answered my cries for help was to redirect my path. While I sat alone in the woods at a spiritual retreat in Wisconsin, the Creator of the universe spoke a clear word: "I want you to listen to your heart and go to your Indian people. I have prepared you for this time in your life." When the voice of truth of all the ages speaks a word, there is no mistaking it.

But I still felt unworthy—not only because of the divorce (in the proceedings of which my ex-wife stated specifically that our daughter was not allowed to live on an Indian reservation) and feelings of failure but also because I was a mixed-blood and had not been raised in a traditional Indian home. I thought I was too much of a thin-blood to be qualified to be in Native ministry. By this time, I knew well the horrors many missions had put on our Indian people, and I felt like I would rather die than become a missionary oppressor again.

Also, I was afraid of rejection. I had always struggled deeply with this fear. Many Native Americans do to one degree or another, but it is especially an issue with mixed-bloods. The rejection coming from the dominant society was one with which I was familiar, and I could live with it. Rejection from Native people, though—for not being Indian enough—was something I wasn't sure I could handle.

I relied on the wisdom of two elder friends, Reeves Nahwooks (Comanche/Kiowa) and his wife, Clydia, who was from a prominent traditional Cherokee family. Through prayers, wisdom, and questioning, they gave me a green light to pursue this sacred path. I soon accepted a job in Anadarko, Oklahoma, as executive director of the Anadarko Christian Center and coordinator for ten Oklahoma Indian churches. Soon my daughter, Leanna, and I were on our way to Anadarko to fill the position. My new position introduced me to members of the Kiowa, Comanche, Apache, Wichita, Caddo, Delaware, Cheyenne, and Arapaho tribes.

Libby, a Kiowa elder, was just one of the people I soon came to know. She and Jake were both in their late seventies and had survived other spouses, and they had recently married. Jake was another well-respected Kiowa elder in the community. Libby's older son had been in ministry, but he had died about one year before I arrived. Losing Bucky was a devastating a loss to her. But Libby said Creator had told her that he would bring her another son. Through ceremonial adoption, I became that son.

My newfound Kiowa family took me under their wing and gave me a sense of acceptance that shielded me from some of my fears. I had a lot to learn about the surrounding cultures. But in these spiritual parents, along with many other elders, friends, and adopted family I had made among several of the tribes, I found excellent teachers.

To my surprise, I became one of Anadarko's most eligible bachelors. Many of the elderly women included me in their matchmaking schemes. I guess they felt sorry for the new single dad in town. I was so busy those first few months that I had no time to consider them seriously. My Kiowa mother was dismayed, as she had looked over the field of prospects and for one reason or another could not find the right match.

In the fall of 1989 I began to hear about a woman in eastern Oklahoma, a relative of one of the church families. That was Edith, who had undergone her own transformation since young adulthood. We'll leave that story, and the story of our dating and marriage, for another time. Suffice it to say that we got married December 23, 1989. As they say, the rest is history.

Love, Trust, and Supporting Others

I (Edith) will pick up the story again here. Randy and I got married after just a little less than three months of knowing each other. People at the time asked me why. I wonder that myself sometimes: How did I know that it was the right thing to do? Why did I trust him when trust was so difficult for me? Early on, I had learned *not* to trust people as a survival strategy. I also didn't think I was worthy of anyone's love—especially the love of Creator. The seed was put into my soul early by hateful missionaries at the church my Baptist grandfather had started. I learned that no matter what I did, I would never be good enough for God.

The answer to my lifelong struggle finally came the morning our baby girl was born. I had always wondered how Randy would ever love our baby, since he did not carry her for nine months. As a mother, I loved her from the moment I found out I was pregnant. But fathers, I wondered: How do they love a child outside their own bodies? But watching closely when Skye was born and was put into Randy's arms, I saw it: this instant, pure love that passed between them. I saw how he looked at her and she at him. It was unmistakable love. That's when it hit me: *that is how Creator loves and cares for me.* From that point on, no matter what happened, I knew Creator was always there for me, along with my ancestors who went before me.

Together Randy and I began to serve the Native American community in Anadarko, Oklahoma, in the western part of the state. Anadarko is often referred to as the Indian capital of the nation. There are seventeen tribes within a forty-mile radius, and Anadarko is often ground zero for Native American activity. Through the years we formed a good number of services for the Indian community. With an unofficial advisory board of elders, we began to make seismic changes to both the denominational churches employing Randy and eventually the community itself.

Shortly after giving birth to Skye, I noticed the struggles of young mothers in the area. I longed to do something to help make life easier for them. I started leading a support group focused on parenting skills, and we started making available diapers, formula, onesies, and other baby supplies. That outreach developed, and we added what we called Baby Day, an event around Christmas. In our community dozens of young mothers, many of whom were single parents, would come to the center where Randy worked to get a huge bundle of baby supplies for their infants and more traditional Christmas gifts, such as toys, for their children. To these moms, it was a great joy and made Christmas feel less needy and more celebratory.

When Randy came on board at the Anadarko Christian Center, it was in rough shape. The center was in a poor neighborhood and included mostly Native, some Black, and some poor Latinx and White families. Randy immediately set about remodeling the place inside and out to breathe new life into it. He raised funds for function, aesthetics, and safety concerns. The community took notice and began to want to hold activities in the building. The houseless and transient community also took notice.

The center already had a voucher system in place for people to get a meal ticket that provided a hamburger, fries, and drink from a local restaurant. Also, on nights when the weather was severe, they could receive a voucher for a local hotel room, which in 1989 cost only $17 (it was not the best hotel in town, but it was warm and dry). These were basic needs, but Randy had the idea that we needed to find a way to help the houseless and transient community feel a sense of dignity. He simply gathered them up for a meeting and asked, "What is it that we could do that would empower you?" The answer was as simple as the question: they wanted a place to shower and wash their clothes. The center had a large gym, so we added showers and washers and dryers.

Anadarko was and is a poor community with an extremely high unemployment rate. We saw the food insecurity around us, and we had room at the center, so we created a food closet. Every Friday people would show up to receive an extension to their groceries. We also distributed food to elders who requested home delivery. We cooperated with the Kiowa Tribe in the summers to host drug- and alcohol-free dances on Saturday nights in our gym. The gym was also used quite heavily for basketball leagues and kids' recreation times. During the school year we had tutoring programs and computer-literacy classes for local children. On some weekends we also took the kids on field trips to expand their horizons. We held an annual winter benefit pow wow to raise funds for an annual summer Indian youth culture camp.

On the church side of things, we created Bible studies, Vacation Bible Schools, a Native pastors training program, and a men's support group, especially for those struggling with alcohol and drugs. We hosted cooperative interchurch services and participated with Cook Indian School through their Theological Education by Extension program, and we began creating and housing a theological library. Randy regularly spoke at churches and often filled in when there was no pastor. He regularly affirmed in his teachings that the cultures of Native people were a gift from Creator. His job was often made more difficult by the churches with paternalistic missionaries—people who spread ugly rumors about him and often created more problems.

Sweat Lodges

Missionaries, by definition, try to convert people. No matter their stripe, they want to change your mind, your heart, and your actions.

Admittedly, this book itself is an endeavor to convert people. If we're honest, we're hoping to convert people away from a Western worldview and to a more Indigenous way of thinking. Again, what is at stake is not just personal well-being but our survival as a species. But like we said earlier, you can't convert to Indigenous values without learning about Indigenous history. That history looks different for each person and tribal group. Learning that history means learning about the harm that settlers and their descendants did and looking toward repair.

When I (Randy) began my work in Anadarko, I offi-
cially requested that the denomination send a letter of regret
and apology for its participation in the residential boarding-
school system. After months of observing the bureaucratic
shuffling, I came to realize that we would never see such a
letter. But the work was not entirely in vain. During that
time, I visited with traditional people from the various
communities to find out their opinions on our missionar-
ies and the legacies of their work among Native communi-
ties. Invariably, they answered that it was the first time the
church had ever asked their opinion on anything.

About half the churches I worked with in Oklahoma
loved me, and the other half wished I had never shown up
and did much in their power to get rid of me. Those were
mostly the ones in more affluent churches—who had been
convinced by missionaries that everything Indian was evil
and there could be no mixing of Native culture and what
they called the gospel. We outright rejected that set of lies
and did much to show the weakness of the argument.

I put together something called the Annual Christ and
Native Culture Conference, where I tried to make room for
reasonable responses to the questions being asked. In the
end, those conferences may have just created a wider gap.
Many Native people had in essence been taught by the mis-
sionaries a lesson that our good friend Richard Twiss used
to characterize this way: "God *loves* you—but he really does
not like you!" In other words, the missionaries believed in a
God who preferred European-based White culture and who
did not tolerate Indian culture, languages, and ceremonies.

In those days, the conversation about the interactions between Indigenous culture and Christianity was just in its embryonic stages, and it was stirring up passions on both sides of the argument. I always checked with a group of local elders before making big decisions about how we were going to work toward the harmonizing of the two sides. They were always amenable to Indian cultural practices.

One issue in particular created quite a stir. I had been invited to several traditional sweat lodges in my first year in Anadarko. One night I had a dream, and the message in the dream was to go to the Cheyenne traditional leaders and ask permission to be trained in a Jesus Sweat. The elders and sweat leaders gave us permission to do so, and within a few months we were trained and began holding our own weekly sweats.

The sweat lodge—or simply the sweat, as it is usually called—is a Native American ceremony of cleansing and purification. A sweat is basically an Indian prayer meeting that takes place in a domed structure, usually built from willow poles, blankets, and canvas tarps. The sweat features considerable variation among Indian tribes. Generally, there are four rounds, each with a different emphasis, in which heated rocks are brought into the lodge. After the door is closed and it is pitch black inside, water is poured over the rocks, filling the darkened interior of the lodge with steam. One purpose of the sweat lodge is to create an environment where the participants are humbled as simple human beings before Creator, creating gratitude and healing.

The sweat lodge became (and sometimes remains) a topic of great controversy among Christians. Having gone through proper protocol with the correct traditional people to receive the right to run this sweat, we encountered no controversy from traditional people. Proper protocol is something we have aways observed when we go to places considered now to be Indian Country. Whenever we go to a new place to speak, we try to find out who the Indigenous tribes are in that area, and we honor them with gifts and ask their permission to be in their land. Such people are gate-keepers, and have been granted by Creator special responsibility for a certain land. This type of protocol was common practice among our Indian people in the old days, and our elders taught us to observe it whenever possible.

Jesus spoke of himself as a gatekeeper. He condemned as thieves and robbers those who try to enter the sheep pen by some other way (John 10:1). We would never think of taking a ceremony or exercising responsibility that was not given us with a blessing attached. This is not our Indian way.

I had followed the instructions in my dream and gone to the proper people to obtain permission for the Jesus Sweat. Today, after more than three decades, we continue to use this ceremony to heal people and change their lives for the better.

But for many people in our Native churches, the merging of what they understood to be the gospel with the sweat lodge was a bridge too far. Many missionaries used to burn sweat lodges to the ground, and some still do. Because of our inclusion of Indian culture in all we did, we had to withstand much opposition from many of the more established Indian churches. As mentioned, past and often present missionaries had declared that almost everything Indian was evil and could have no place in the church. In these churches, the drum was replaced by the organ, the circle and outdoor arbor were replaced by square church buildings with steeples, and Euro-based Christian culture became the standard for Native Americans. Our Indian churches are often what I call a poor imitation of a bad model.

Part of the reason our Native American people submitted to this form of ethnocentrism and oppression had to do with our traditional Indigenous values surrounding honor, respect, and gratitude. The earliest Native American followers of the Jesus Road were often quite grateful to hear a message of God's sacrificial love for them. The missionaries who brought the message were, for the most part, well meaning, having sacrificed much themselves to come to Indian Country. Many of our elders, in their gratitude, considered it rude and disrespectful to argue with the missionaries over such things. They did not want to offend those who had given up so much. As a result, some of those first Native followers of Jesus began to disregard their own cultural practices altogether, while others would tiptoe around to pow wows and ceremonies, hoping the missionaries would not find out. This created a binary that manifests itself among Christian Indians today. In the minds of most of the missionaries, the message was simple: choose to be Christian or choose to be Indian, but you can't be both.

For us to enter over a hundred years of a strong historic missionary tradition and proclaim another way was perilous. But we knew we had a group of elders on our side, as well as basic human decency and respect for the cultures. Although we suffered slander and abuse from some of the churches, we simply knew we were on the right path.

That path also led us to organize a grassroots group to deal with the many civil injustices our Native people were suffering. The Anadarko police had a practice of arresting an unusually high number of people of color on Fridays, which meant they could not be arraigned at least until Monday. This tactic meant people spent extra days in jail—which created extra income for the system.

As we began to hear stories from prisoners—of abuse and racism, of beatings and sometimes even death—we knew we had to do something. I began attending arraignments just to let the judge know outsiders were watching. We also formed a social-justice organization and began having meetings to organize the local community. We became involved in several serious cases of overt racism, discrimination, and even a murder trial. We also reported the terrible conditions of the jail to the local newspaper and the county health commission, and they found thirty-one violations. The county jail was given two weeks to make the corrections on the threat of releasing prisoners.

Every so often our actions were highlighted—negatively— in the opinion page of the local newspaper. As you might imagine, the local good-old-boy network was not happy with us—especially when we exposed the injustices and discrimination of the city, county, and local electric co-op, which were the largest employers in the county. While over 50 percent of the residents of the area were people of color, none of these entities employed more than 3 percent people of color. The entire system was rigged to fail for Black, Indigenous, and other people of color. We even exposed the police department for discrimination in hiring.

Life became dangerous for us. Late at night, on several occasions, pickup trucks with their lights off followed my car on the country road leading to our home. We received threatening calls as well. We knew we were being targeted and warned.

6

BEAR DREAMS

Returning to Our Indigenous Roots

Some dreams can emerge from material in our subconscious—ideas we haven't dealt with that surface in the night. Some dreams result from too much lasagna before bedtime. But sometimes dreams are gifts from Creator.

I (Randy) am a dreamer. During those bleak days of being targeted for our work in exposing the police department for its racism, I had a series of dreams. I believe they were meant to prepare me for a change that was about to happen. These dreams were very spiritual, and they all centered on bears.

Some tribes consider bear dreams to be so sacred that you should not talk about them to a person who has not experienced a bear dream—one who has not had bear medicine. Among the Cherokee is a story of a particular clan that became prideful and began to live like hermits, all alone in the woods, away from the rest of the people. Eventually they grew hairy and turned into bears.

Knowing these stories, I took my bear dreams seriously. In each dream, I was in the woods, hunting for a bear. I knew that in many tribes, bears represented a person's greatest fears. In each dream I would corner the bear, and as I drew close to shoot, the bear would begin talking to me. Each time the bears told me that I really did not want to shoot *them*, because they could tell me where the biggest, meanest bear lived. *He* was the one I was really after. This same dream occurred three times over a period of weeks. Recurrent dreams are often very significant spiritually.

Then came the fourth and final bear dream. In the dream I found myself on a long hunt, having found the trail of the largest, meanest bear, which I and everyone else feared. When at last I made the bear come out of his cave, I saw the bear was old, bent over, losing his hair, and somewhat toothless.

In the dream I laughed at myself. *This* was the bear that had terrified me? I told the bear I would allow him to live, since he could do no more harm to himself or anyone else.

In a very real way, those dreams were about my own identity as a Keetoowah, and they gave me courage to face some of my lifelong fears. The big, bad bear was my fear of rejection from my own people. I had identified as Cherokee, and yet I had never lived among my own tribe, where the old beliefs, stories, and ceremonies were in many ways still intact. At the time, I did not ask a lot of questions of people or share the dream, because it seemed too sacred to talk about to anyone who might trivialize my quest. Though I did not know it then, soon enough I would be moving to Cherokee Country.

Considering the many threats against us in the wake of our work for justice, and given our longing for safety for our elementary school–aged daughter, Leanna, and a newborn daughter, Skye, we decided that moving from Anadarko to Muscogee, Oklahoma, was the right choice. We still sometimes wonder whether we made the best choice. We left so many good friends and family in western Oklahoma. But we could also see we were being targeted by forces beyond our capacity to protect our family.

My new job at Bacone Indian College was on the other side of Oklahoma, in Cherokee Country. Eastern Oklahoma is an entirely different world from western Oklahoma. Western Oklahoma's Indian culture is predominately Plains Indian culture. The tribes in eastern Oklahoma were moved there by the United States from the eastern parts of the country, which included the Cherokee, my tribal roots, and the Choctaw, Edith's mother's people.

I found much acceptance among my own people in eastern Oklahoma. Learning the Cherokee language and more of our history was a delight, and we attended traditional gatherings such as Stomp Dance and other ceremonies. I felt very much at home, especially learning more of our Keetoowah story. Edith was also learning more about her mother's people.

During this time, we also faced many personal disappointments. While our daughter Skye's birth came about smoothly, it took years of frustration to have another child. Anyone who has gone through the pain of infertility will understand the disappointment of which we speak. After years of distress about having another child, our church decided to hold a special sweat lodge ceremony for us and pray for our healing and fertility. About a month later we discovered those prayers had worked, and Edith was pregnant with our second child, Young-Joseph. But things did not go well with the pregnancy, and we were told to expect the loss of the child we had tried so hard to bring into this world.

At the college, I was encountering struggles and problems too numerous to go into in these pages. The short version is that I was learning, once again, that speaking truth to power about systemic racism had serious consequences, which in this case included losing my job. The summer of 1994 was a lonely and desperate time for our family. We had begun to lose confidence in our denomination as well, realizing that the denomination would never be able to go as far as we wanted to go concerning Indigenous people and cultural practices. The strain in the relationship was apparent, and more and more we began to find a sense of deeper spirituality among our Native traditional people than among Christians. I had no job prospects, though I had applied for many positions. Overnight, it seemed, we were jobless, expecting a child we were told would die, and we would soon be houseless.

I had been taking a nighttime course at the community college on traditional Cherokee plants and medicines, something for which I'd always had a passion. The teacher was a traditional Cherokee and a nurse practitioner. On the final night, the teacher asked me to stay after class. She told me she had watched my passion about the course material and had shared it with her mentor, William Smith, who was probably the most respected Cherokee traditional medicine person in Oklahoma. She said Smith wanted to talk with me to see whether I'd be interested in becoming his new apprentice.

An opportunity like this only comes once in a lifetime. But by then, we had already found a job and committed to work in Nevada, and the move would happen just two weeks later. I had to regretfully decline the offer. I had a family to take care of, now with another child on the way, and the apprenticeship did not pay anything. Sadly, there was no other choice except to say no.

We often wonder what would have happened if we were able to work things out. I would have been steeped in my Cherokee traditions and in that community. Instead, we headed farther west, to Carson City, Nevada. By now, we were reclaiming our God-given Indigenous spirituality. We were on the path toward Eloheh. But we didn't know how we would fare in the future.

Deepening Indigeneity

Shortly after our arrival in Nevada, an obstetrician told me (Edith) that the baby was no longer in danger. Our son Ruben Young-Joseph Woodley was born in January 1995. He was a healthy boy of nine pounds, but during his birth, he got stuck in the birth canal with the cord wrapped around his neck. At first, he wasn't breathing and was blue to the lack of oxygen. Although I did not see what was happening, Randy was right there, saw the whole thing, and began praying. After a few minutes Ruben Young-Joseph started breathing and pinked up quickly. Extreme gratitude overwhelmed us.

Randy's new job was to pastor the Tahoe Indian Parish churches. Randy never had a desire to be a pastor, and he certainly did not want to be a missionary again. He had informed the denomination that he would not go as a missionary but as a person who answered primarily to the people there, not to the denomination. The denomination cut their financial support in half, and later we would discover their moral support was cut as well.

Out of a church of seventeen people, only two were Indians, and both were over seventy-five years old, having been a matron and patron at the boarding school. During the interview time, we spoke with community members in the neighborhood and heard several Indians in town repeat similar words to us about the church. The feeling was that the only time any Indian wanted to enter that church was to be either married or buried. To build trust in the Native community, we'd have to overcome its long negative reputation and history.

In addition to its many current struggles, the congregation had a storied history. It met in the same church building that abused Indian students were forced to attend while they were students at the Stewart Indian Boarding School. Once again, we were faced with the legacy of the residential boarding-school system that had so decimated my own father's life as well as the life of my grandmother. It didn't help that the church was still named after the school. Why would any Native person want to come there now?

There were also some personal losses. We had experienced many wounds of friendly fire from our beloved Christian brothers and sisters and had learned how to love them anyway, hoping one day that they would love us back. During this stressful time, there was also incredible personal pain in that we lost two pregnancies, one a miscarriage at thirteen weeks and the other a stillbirth at thirty-four weeks. We did get to hold our son Josiah Samuel Woodley for just a moment after the doctor delivered him. Randy bravely held the funeral service, and Josiah is now buried in the children's section of a cemetery in Carson City.

After these two losses, Creator blessed us again with another son in 1998. As with all our children, he is a special blessing. There is an old Cherokee story about the redbird returning the age of beauty back to the people after a dark time. We named our son John-Dalton Redbird Woodley.

We now have four children, all grown up, and at the time of this writing, six grandchildren. We have a marriage built on love and trust. The miscarriages and child losses along the way nearly leveled us. Life has certainly had its share of difficulties, but we feel blessed. We thank Creator and pray for our little family every day.

The First Dog Soldier

It took about four years for us to steady the church in Carson City. At first, we became a multicultural, multiracial church with a little Indianness, which caused the membership to grow to over one hundred. Then, as we became more culturally Native American, a lot of the non-Indians left. Then we had some ideas about how it should go culturally, but when new changes were made, some of the White people, who still had a considerable amount of political and financial power, began complaining. This became a pivotal time in our lives.

Yes, we were very culturally Native—on the outside. Our chairs sat in a circle with the big drum in the middle. People could sage themselves upon entrance with an eagle feather. We sang Indian songs in the circle. But still, something was missing. All this time, power was vested in the church council (council seemed like a nice Indian word), but the council was not in line with the people.

One of the elders in our community was instrumental in moving us toward a fuller spirituality and away from religion. Randy had first met Stanley outside the county jail. He had been asked to go pray for a Native man who had just shot and killed his wife's lover. The man's mother called the church and asked whether Randy was the Indian pastor who prayed with sage and eagle feathers. He answered yes, and she asked him to go pray for her son, who had just been arrested.

The jailers would not allow him to light the sage inside the jail, so Randy said he would pray the Indian way outside. As Randy was praying in the four directions, with his eagle feather and sage, he noticed three Native men leaning against the side of the jail, having a smoke. They all wore black leather jackets, sunglasses, and berets tilted sideways. He was pretty sure they were with the American Indian Movement, since they dressed the part. After Randy finished, the elder of the group, a short man in his sixties with long silver hair, walked up to Randy and spoke.

"What are you up to?" he asked.

Randy replied, "I'm praying for Dennis out here, because they won't let me light this sage inside."

"Oh, those sons of bitches," Stanley said. "I'm Dennis's cousin. Who are you?"

"I'm the pastor of the Baptist church," Randy replied.

Stanley was surprised, and he took a small step back. "You'll never catch me inside a church," he said. "I had enough of that shit in boarding school."

"Maybe you would come to my sweat?" Randy said. He had started sweats again by that time, with the blessing of the local people and a dream where he was told to go ahead.

Again, Stanley was taken aback. "Uh, maybe you'll come to mine?" he replied.

"Sure, just give me a call at the church," Randy said.

A few weeks later Stanley did call. He left a message saying they were having a sweat the following day, a Saturday evening, and left his address. That was one hot sweat! Randy thinks they were purposely trying to test him to see what he was made of. He lasted the whole time, with a lot of prayer. The next sweat Randy held, Stanley was there. Eventually, Randy attended Native American church services (Peyote church), pow wows, and other ceremonies at Stanley's invite. Randy even become one of the singers with all those guys in the sweat with their drum group.

Stanley became instrumental in making sure we did everything the right way ceremonially. He became an unofficial church leader and elder in many ways, and he never did stop cussing like a sailor. Stanley's family and ours became very close, spending many holidays and a lot of other times together.

In our final year at Carson City, Stanley developed hip cancer. Randy often took him for his treatments. While he was in the hospital one night, late, he called and asked Randy to come pray for him. It was a very sacred time. Randy prayed over him with an eagle fan and sang an Indian song of comfort. They had prayed and sang together in so many sweat ceremonies before, but this time something was different.

Later, on one of the trips to his treatments, Stanley asked Randy whether he could have the water ceremony. Randy explained that this water ceremony—that is, baptism—is for people who follow Jesus. Stanley made it clear that he had met the spirit-man Jesus the night Randy had prayed for him in the hospital.

The church was packed for the water ceremony—not with many church folks but with many of the traditional people in the community and Stanley's relatives. Stanley sat up front in a chair. He used the bucket and ladle that were always used in sweat lodge. Stanley held up four eagle feathers going in the four directions as Randy poured the ladle of water over his head. There was not a dry eye in the house.

Later we came to realize Stanley taught us more than we knew. Some of it was not fully realized until after we left Nevada. He and his family gave us their friendship, and that was the most precious gift of all. He taught us that being Christian was largely a project of the West. He taught us that Jesus is spirit, and we all have access to him and all the other good spirits. He taught us theology as well: good, Indigenous theology that was a plain as day after we thought about it.

One day Randy was meeting with a group of visiting pastors at our church, and Stanley happened to walk in. Randy had shared with them earlier about the water ceremony. One of the pastors realized who Stanley was and came over to greet him with a hug. "I hear you are a Christian now!" he said.

Stanley was not what one would call huggable. He backed up quickly and said, "I ain't no Christian!"

All the pastors looked at Randy in surprise.

"Oh," said Stanley, with a quick smile. "You mean: do I follow Jesus, *hota matah maya*, the first Dog Soldier? Yeah. But don't call me no Christian."

Stanley had made something crystal clear in less than a minute. Dog soldiers were a select group of Cheyenne warriors, and there were similar warrior societies among the Plains tribes, such as the Lakota Kit Foxes, Shoshone White Knives, and Kiowa Real Dogs. These groups would stake themselves to the land with a long sash and forfeit their lives as an act of sacrifice, protection, and courage for the sake of their people. By calling Jesus the first Dog Soldier, Stanley was suggesting that Jesus's bravery and sacrifice was for the people—and that's what being traditional is all about. Jesus should be honored for his sacrifice, but Jesus didn't come to make Christians. He came to show us what it means to live in harmony and love for the people.

Following Stanley's lead, we began to no longer think of ourselves as Christians. We were people following both the Native American traditional road and the way of Jesus. We understood, largely influenced by Stanley and several other friends in Nevada, how a much fuller spirituality helped us walk with spiritual integrity.

Life in the community was full and beautiful for our final several years in Nevada. The structure of our church had changed so that everyone had a voice, and no one took themselves too seriously. Our outdoor talking circle began drawing many Native Americans from the community. Finally, after over four years of struggle, we had a real Indian church.

We changed the name of the church to reflect the original local Indian reference to the location: we became the Eagle Valley Church. We also stopped using the word *Christian* to describe ourselves. It was the Christians who brought all the oppression and misery, hand in hand with the US government. It was a handle no one wanted, so we simply began following Jesus in our own Native ways, using our own ceremonies and stories. As a spiritual leader who taught truth, Jesus seemed to carry no problematic associations. Was he God in flesh? Our people believed in many manifestations of the Great Mystery on Earth, and no one had trouble believing Jesus as spirit or speaking with him. Doctrine became what we did in love to others, not what we thought was orthodox.

The Eagle Valley Church grew in numbers and depth of loving relationships. We became a model for other Native American churches in the United States and Canada. With all the national attention we were drawing just by being ourselves, more requests came in for us to speak, and more people wanted us to come visit. After six years, the church released us to work only half-time and go speak half-time. Several capable leaders were taking responsibility for the operations at the church by that time. After working at the church part-time and traveling part-time just became too difficult, we all decided together that it was time to leave the church to pursue the bigger vision of Eloheh.

Just before leaving, we had one more thing we needed to do.

Boarding-School Healing

Our church had been on a journey toward Indigenous values, such as the ones we will look at in the rest of the chapters. Groups and individuals alike can make the journey toward Eloheh. For both groups and individuals interested in the Harmony Way, however, it's important to not only learn Indigenous values but also to acknowledge the harm and legacy of Western values.

Since the Stewart Indian Baptist Church had been part of the oppression of Native Americans due to its affiliation with the Stewart Indian Boarding School, a name change was not enough. We decided, before leaving, with the help of several other Native leaders, to have a time of healing and address the issues surrounding the boarding school.

Over the years, we had heard so many horrific stories from survivors who had attended the boarding school as children: of torture and abuse and starvation. It was time to expose the issues and allow those people who had attended to speak of it as they chose.

The meetings were held on a Friday evening and Saturday. The Friday night event was hosted at one of the two non-Native churches that asked to be part of the healing process. The agenda for Friday evening was to honor the elders who had attended the school with a good meal, to watch a short film about the horrors of boarding schools, and to allow anyone who attended the school or was a relative of someone who attended to share, if they desired to do so. Saturday was designated as a time of ceremonial healing and honoring the elders with gifts.

For people from the two non-Native churches that helped to host the event, seeing the film on Friday was an epiphany. It revealed a story that Native families know all too well but that many of the non-Native guests had not encountered. Unfortunately, when Indian stories become too sad, you can always count on a White person, someone who is uncomfortable with the depth of hurt being shared, to try to gloss things over or rationalize the offenses of the perpetrators. "Surely it wasn't as bad as all that," someone will say, and someone else will add, "Well, I'm sure those teachers and staff members *meant* well." The other thing we often observed was a White person who had learned a bit of our history talk so authoritatively—and at length—that the Native participants couldn't get a word in edgewise. We had seen this happen in the past, and we were not going to allow this to happen this time.

Randy was the moderator of the event, and he set a hard-and-fast rule: if you were not a student at the boarding school or a relative of a boarding-school victim, your role was to listen, not speak. Though some White participants tried to add their two cents over and over again, Randy strictly enforced that rule. Boarding-school survivors and their family members were granted the space to tell their stories. As they shared, we all learned of the trauma they'd undergone and the resilience they'd demonstrated. We once again learned the ways that Native values have survived across the millennia, despite all the attempts to extinguish them.

You have now learned the contours of our stories. We turn now to a chapter-by-chapter exploration of the ten Native values that can lead us all toward well-being. These are harmony, respect, accountability, history, humor, authenticity, equality, community, balance, and generosity.

If these ideas are new to you, and if you have had little contact with Indigenous stories, people, and ways of life, we suggest you take a posture of listening and learning. When we encounter and get excited about ideas that are new to us, it can be easy to imagine we are experts right away and to begin preaching to others about them. But we invite you to encounter these values as listeners and learners, and to consider silence as the best immediate response.

So together we will look at the stories and practices we've learned from friends and kin from across different Indigenous tribes and nations—people who are traveling along the Harmony Way.

7

HARMONY

Seeking Peace

The elders say there was a time the Cherokee people were misusing their resources. They were disrespecting the animals by not using all parts of the animal when they hunted and by not being grateful to them for giving their lives. These were evil days indeed.

The animal people held a council to figure out how to protect themselves from the evil that had come on them from the once-grateful Cherokee. They decided to get revenge on the Cherokee people by giving them various diseases. After many Cherokees had died of smallpox, influenza, and measles, the remaining people finally asked the animals to forgive them. They pleaded with the animals,

"Please, we will become grateful and kill only what we will eat." But the animals would not recant. They decided to continue their revenge.

All the while, the plant people were watching. They felt sorry for the dying Cherokee. So the plants held a council, in which they agreed to provide medicine for the Cherokee. Each night, as the Cherokees slept, the plants would come to them in their dreams and show them how to use the plants to heal the diseases that the animals had brought on them. In their dreams, the plants sent them instructions for finding the plant medicines to remedy their various ailments.

The Cherokees began to get well. They found the medicinal plants that helped them heal, and they were grateful.

Afterward, the Cherokee council, the animal council, and the plant council all came together. They decided together what ways the people could act in order to maintain harmony and balance in the world. The Cherokees agreed to kill only what they absolutely needed. They also agreed to sing a song before hunting and kill only an animal that gave itself to the hunter. They agreed that the Cherokees would put tobacco down on the ground and say a prayer of thanks to any animal that they killed and to any plant that would be harvested for food, medicine, warmth, or shelter. Creator was happy with the Cherokees once again, because harmony was restored among all created things.

The story reveals an important point: that is, in Native American understandings, harmony is the key to all happiness, health, and well-being. Harmony is the hallmark of

Native American spirituality, and it must involve the whole community of creation. Our lives are governed by harmony.

Harmony was much easier to maintain prior to the European invasion. Much in our lives and in society is out of balance because the government and Christian church attempted to dissolve all our traditional structures and ceremonies. It's difficult now to get things back into harmony.

When Euro-Americans hear statements such as these— that harmony is a value that Indigenous peoples hold in common—they sometimes cast them aside as an unrealistic or nostalgic view of the Native American past. Many descendants of settlers have a difficult time believing that Native Americans prefer the values of their own past to the values of the Europatricene. But these statements don't reflect a type of Native American utopianism. They simply acknowledge that there can be no way forward unless we reclaim the ways that worked so well for us in the past.

This connection to the past is strong and pervasive among Native Americans. Vine Deloria Jr. said, "Even the most severely eroded Indian community today still has a substantial fragment of the old ways left, and these ways are to be found in the Indian family. Even the badly shattered families preserve enough elements of kinship so that whatever the experiences of the young, there is a sense that life has some unifying principles that can be discerned through experience that guides behavior. This feeling, and it is a strong emotional feeling towards the world that transcends beliefs and information, continues to gnaw at American Indians throughout their lives."

Deloria speaks of "unifying principles," which are essentially the same as what we call values of the Harmony Way. In this chapter we look at the first of those ten values, harmony, which is foundational to everything. We will look at the remaining nine values in the following chapters.

But Deloria also is addressing a specific feeling that connects Indians to the past: a feeling that "gnaws" at us. Native Americans experience cognitive dissonance because we must live under colonial systems and values, which have become powerful, ubiquitous, and totalizing. Meanwhile, we have watched as our values are subjugated. As we move forward, we will continue to discover the importance of restoring harmony in our lives.

Seek to Maintain Balance in All of Life

We have learned from our people that when things get out of balance, it is our human responsibility to bring things back into harmony. According to our Cherokee beliefs, human beings, while they are on Earth, are responsible to maintain harmony and to restore harmony when it becomes broken. One of the ways this is done among our tribal people is by keeping our traditional ceremonies, such as the Navajo way of harmony *Hózhóón*, or "beauty-way ceremony." Many other Native American tribes have a similar understanding. Even in our sweat lodge ceremony, balance is a key. Near the end of the ceremony, if the mood is too solemn, we use the fourth round to tell funny stories or jokes. Or if the mood during the sweat was light, we might make some serious admonitions before ending the ceremony.

Even if your ancestors did not have ceremonies that you can revive—or if they did but you don't know what they were—there are other ways to seek to maintain harmony. Although the two of us have failed at this many times, harmony is the aim to which we aspire and the center to which we always return. We have raised our family trying to uphold harmony as a principle. For example, money has never been our primary concern. Whether we were employed by someone else or living by the generosity of donors, we have always limited our income to the low- to medium-income levels listed in each county in which we lived at the time.

Another example of harmony lived out is contentment. We have learned to be content driving older cars. At the time of this writing, we drive a 2015 Subaru Outback and a 2002 Dodge Ram pickup. We also grow our own food and share it with others. When we had animals on the farm or obtained wild game through hunting, we maintained proper ceremony, butchered our own animals, and shared our gain. At each place we live, we always leave room for the wild animals and birds and other creatures to remain unmolested by setting aside sections of land for them. All these examples are about harmony and balance.

We are not bragging or setting ourselves up as better than anyone else. But we want you to know that trying to live in harmony results in practical commitments. When we center harmony in our lives, we learn to maintain a balance in life and become generous with what we have.

We have learned from our elders and the teachings of other people from many tribes that harmony is the key to a life well lived. To help you understand how central this way of harmony is to our Indigenous people, we will share with you what various other Indigenous people say about it.

Remember That All Things Are Connected

Within the lifestyle of maintaining harmony and balance lies an understanding of interconnectedness. Traditional Native Americans feel a sense of interconnectedness at a deep level. We connect the physical to the emotional to the spiritual, and ourselves to one another and the natural world. We connect the whole community of creation to our civic responsibilities. In Indigenous thinking, there is no such thing as separation of one part of our life from another.

An example of the interconnectedness is found among the Lakota. Some of the most basic structures to Lakota life were the warrior societies. Yet there existed (and remains) a lifeway of harmony, expressed through a belief in the interrelatedness of all things. This included, for the Lakota, all the Sioux tribes, other tribes, and other humans, as well as all the animals, birds, insects, plants, and the rest of the community of creation. They express this interrelatedness through the words of a common prayer: *mitakuye oyasin.* Here is what Clara Sue Kidwell, Homer Noley, and George

Tinker write in *A Native American Theology*: "A translation of *mitakuye oyasin* would better read: 'For all the above me and below me and around me things.' That is, for all my relations. . . . It is this understanding of inter-relatedness, of balance and mutual respect of the different species in the world, that characterizes what we might call Indian people's greatest gift to Amer-Europeans and to the Amer-European understanding of creation at this time of world ecological crisis."

Giving credence to this idea—that all people and things are related to one another—opens us to immense possibility. What if we once again saw ourselves as family to the whole community of creation? We must come to the realization that all the world is our relative.

By realizing the connectedness of humankind to all animal and plant life, the Lakota believe that we become aware of new possibilities for preserving all living things. In humanity's dependence on the Earth, the Lakota and others believe we can learn to sustain our planet and can find fresh prospects for nurturing food, conserving water, and developing renewable energy. All this and more is contained in their two simple prayer words: *mitakuye oyasin*, "All my relations."

Among the Iroquoian peoples of the Six Nations came one they called the Peacemaker, a person who united the tribes during terrible times of turmoil. The Peacemaker knew the interconnectedness at the root of all things. The Six Nations still live today according to the law and teachings of the Peacemaker, also known as Deganawida, whose view of harmonious living is consistent with those already mentioned.

Tadodaho, also known as Chief Leon Shenandoah, commented:

> The teachings are very good. The most important thing is that each individual must treat all others, all the people who walk on Mother Earth, including every nationality, with kindness. That covers a lot of ground. It doesn't apply only to my people. I must treat everyone I meet the same. When people turn their thoughts to the Creator, they give the Creator power to enter their minds and bring good thoughts. The most difficult part of this is that the Creator desired that there be no bloodshed among human beings and that there be peace, good relations, and always a good mind.

Like the Lakota concept of *mitakuye oyasin*, the Iroquois philosophy seeks to bring all people together in one accord by recognizing that all people and creation are interconnected. Chief Shenandoah shares how this interconnectedness is related to the Harmony Way. "In explaining the good news to a chief named Degaihogen, Deganawidah presented a vision of a world community," Chief Shenandoah recounts. "'What shall we be like,' Degaihogen had asked, 'when this reason and righteousness and justice and health have come?' 'In truth,' replied Deganawidah, 'reason brings righteousness, and reason is power that works among all minds alike. When once reason is established, all the minds of all mankind will be in a state of health and peace. It will be as if there were but a single person.'"

The "reason" to which Chief Leon Shenandoah refers is the sense of interconnectedness at the root of a harmonious existence. This way of living is substantiated among various Native peoples, so many of whom have a common value of harmony. Ojibway elder Eddie Benton Banai writes, "Today, we should use these ancient teachings to live our lives in harmony with the plan that the Creator gave us. We are to do these things if we are to be natural people of the universe."

Benton Banai connects the past and the present through Harmony Way teachings, calling them "natural." He concludes his book by referring to the Ojibway concept of harmony in their own language: "There are yet more teachings that can teach us how to live *ni-noo-do-da-di-win* [harmony] with the creation."

Imagine Harmony as a Hoop

The connectedness within the Harmony Way—the harmony that holds everything together—is most often represented symbolically as a circle or a hoop. Our friend and relative Fern Cloud, a Dakota woman who is a hoop dancer and runs an organization called Mending the Hoop, notes the tendency of people operating out of a Western worldview to see the Harmony Way as a philosophy. "*Wo 'dakota* [Harmony] is not a philosophy," she tells us. "It's a path of life we do, looking at what Creator gave us in that whole circle of life and living it."

To Fern, and to us and many other Native Americans, this point is crucial. A philosophy can be *believed*, but the Harmony Way must be *lived*. It requires not only belief but action, which aligns itself with the whole of the universe.

The list of tribes whose overall lifeways promote a similar view of harmony might include every North American Native tribal group. This idea is evidenced by a common active spirituality, expressed by common symbols, often including the eagle feather; the burning of plants such as sage, sweetgrass, and cedar; and even the most ordinary symbol: the circle.

Canadian Cree theologian Stan McKay makes the connection between the sacred circle and the harmony present among our Indigenous peoples. He writes:

The image of living on the Earth in harmony with creation and therefore the Creator, is a helpful image for me. . . . Each day we are given is for thanksgiving for the Earth. We are to enjoy it and share it in service of others. This is the way to grow in unity and harmony. . . . It allows for diversity within the unity of the Creator. . . . There are many teachings in the aboriginal North American Nations that use the symbol of the circle. It is the symbol for the inclusive caring community, where individuals are respected, and inter-dependence is recognized. In the wider perspective it symbolizes the natural order of creation in which human beings are part of the whole circle of life. Aboriginal spiritual teachers speak of the re-establishment of the balance between human beings and the whole of creation, as a mending of the hoop.

The circle or hoop is found in nearly all tribes as a powerful representation of the Earth, life, seasons, and cycles of maturity. This symbol is found in cliff drawings, called petroglyphs, and other ancient sources. Many ceremonies, such as Sundance, pow wow, Native American Church (peyotism), and Ghost Dance, are fashioned intentionally in a circle.

The circle is also a common shape in nature. Trees, rocks, whirlpools, tornadoes, and flowers all bear a resemblance to circular objects. In general, right angles do not naturally occur in nature without assistance from a human being.

Do circles show up in your life? When you notice circles in nature and in settings around you, try calling to mind the value of harmony. Remind yourself every day that all things are connected, that all people and things are your relatives. How might that change how you see the world?

Seek Peace

Descendants of settlers often stereotype Indians as violent savages. Perhaps one of the most ubiquitous harms done to Native Americans has been the creation of the "Hollywood

Indian," what Vine Deloria calls "the Indians of the American imagination."

We can all recall scenes from one of the most successful genres of film and literature in American pop culture: the Western. There, larger than life, the bloodthirsty "savages" lie in wait to attack poor White settlers, who are portrayed as just minding their own business. In the early 1970s, great strides were made in understanding the reasons the Indians in the movies were attacking the settlers, à la *Little Big Man*, *Jeremiah Johnson*, *Billy Jack*, and others.

This sympathy led many people to begin linking Indians to other popular social concerns, such as caring for the Earth. The romanticized image of the Native became powerful—as if somehow, by their very essence, Indians are spokespersons for the natural world. We want to assure you: Native Americans do not hold a patent on understanding the natural world. Non-Indigenous people, though, have forgotten their own indigeneity and need to be reminded by those Indigenous peoples who are not as far removed from their relationship with the Earth.

Unfortunately, neither stereotype—warring savage or romanticized environmentalist—gives attention to our robust philosophies of socioreligious harmony or concepts of tolerance, nonviolence, and peacemaking, of which there are many. On this continent, before settlers arrived, harmonious ways of coming together and restoring relationships developed. War was bad for everyone. When people went to war, the trading of goods halted. Children could no longer play freely. Women could not go out on their own. So the Indigenous peoples of Turtle Island did all that was in their power to maintain the peace. The sources confirming these commonly held principles of harmony among Native Americans are many and varied in nuance. But it can be stated, without great disputation, that most North American Indigenous tribes held to a lifeway of harmony and peacemaking.

Even among tribes with a reputation as the most warlike there existed striking counterbalances in their structure and philosophy of war. This way of thinking was expressed in 1876 by revered Brule' Lakota Chief Spotted Tail, who said, "When people come to trouble, it is better for both parties to come together without arms and talk it over and find some peaceful way to settle it."

Another example is that of the Cheyenne peace chiefs. According to the teachings of Sweet Medicine, the most revered Cheyenne teacher and prophet, all forty-four chiefs among them must be committed to peace. Even today, Sweet Medicine's words are repeated at the inauguration of every new chief. Here's how author Stanley Hoig recounts it: "'Listen to me carefully,' Sweet Medicine advised, 'and truthfully follow up my instructions. You chiefs are peacemakers. Though your son might be killed in front of your tepee, you should take a pipe and smoke. Then you should be called an honest chief. . . . If strangers come, you are the ones to give presents to them and invitations. When you meet someone, he comes to your teepee, asking for anything, give it to him. Never refuse.'"

The structure of the Cheyenne was such that these words (strikingly reminiscent of the teaching of Jesus concerning loving one's enemies) are still valued as the highest form of response to both personal tragedy and the needs of others. In the Cheyenne system, the one who lives according to these teachings is of all people most honored.

In the history of Cherokee people, war and peace were seen as crucial sides of a great balance. Two separate councils maintained this balance. The White Council, sometimes called the Peace Council, was responsible for domestic affairs within the village. The Red Council, or War Council, dealt with foreign concerns and disputes. The White Council government was the status quo until issues concerning foreign affairs emerged. At that time, the White Council stepped down until the issues of foreign affairs, such as war, were resolved, at which time the White Council would be reinstated.

Besides wars, there were several common, less violent alternatives the Cherokee used to resolve conflict such as disputes over hunting grounds. These included the two quarreling tribal groups playing a stickball match, the winner takes all. The Cherokee and other tribes also practiced the giving of gifts to make peace, adoption and marriage ceremonies to people from the other tribe, and the sending and receiving of ambassadors. All of these were decentralized, multilevel peacemaking efforts.

Perhaps the most striking image of Native American peacemaking comes from the Peacemaker story from the

Iroquois Confederacy. According to our friend Adrian Jacobs, when Hiawatha stood before the Great Cannibal, who had killed Hiawatha's last child, instead of hatred he had compassion. An unexpected move on the part of Hiawatha exhibits this compassion: Hiawatha took a comb and began to comb the snakes out of the Great Cannibal's hair. The Cannibal was immediately converted to a peaceful existence. The dramatic picture is one of peace. Degoni-widah, the Peacemaker, then installed the Great Cannibal as a great chief of peace.

Jacobs then tells how this remarkable transformation affected the whole Confederacy:

> These two people were an influence in the original five nations, teaching us to listen to each other, pain and grief and death—this condolence is like coming home—to be with people who dignify you and embrace and they ceased the cannibalism. I can just see the whole society opening to this peace, which is, with this conversion of the chief, turns the whole community around. Hiawatha and Cannibal conversion—sees what he is doing is wrong, and the revelation comes through this peacemaker. He is made the head of this confederacy . . . even though everyone has a voice. But what is foundational is that people can turn from this other way of imbalance or being out of harmony, and what you gain is the embrace of each other in peace.

Because of all these teachings from our own tribes and others, we try to live as peacekeepers and peacemakers. To do otherwise would bring us out of harmony.

When our family lived in Carson City, Nevada, a group of eleven Indian youth, some connected to our church, were accused of murdering a Salvadoran gang member at an after-party. Sparing you the details, we'll just say we believe they were innocent and wrongly accused. The town of Carson City became expectant with fright and animosity toward these youth.

Because I (Randy) had already made friends with Victor, a Latin American pastor associated with the family of the leader of the gang who had been killed, I made a call to him. Together we wondered how we could begin to heal our community. Victor let us know that the wife of the person killed wished to accompany his body back to El Salvador for a burial in his hometown. Our Indian church took up an offering, and Victor and I delivered the gift—in an amount that would cover all her travel expenses—to her in person. The following Sunday Victor spoke at our church, and I at his.

When the Native youth went to court for their arraignment, there were rumors that there would be violence. Snipers took up positions on nearby rooftops, and police in shields and riot gear separated the people attending on the outside steps. The wide middle section of steps was taped with yellow tape reading, "Do Not Cross." Native Americans were sent to the right-side steps and Latinx people to the left-side steps. It makes sense, from a Western worldview, to keep the two groups completely separated. But when Victor and I arrived together and saw what was happening, we set up a plan. I crossed over to the left side and Victor to the right—the opposite sides of where we were told to go. People from both sides erupted in loud cheers and applause. We sent a message of solidarity and peace, of harmony and interrelatedness, that day.

This is the wisdom and teaching of our ancestors: people who were proud warriors but who would, under almost any circumstances, prefer peace. We don't see those aspects of strategic peacemaking in Hollywood movies about Indians or in the stories told about our people in books.

We continue to include peacemaking as a part of our teaching of the Harmony Way. This has included trying to repair the breach between traditional Native people and Christians. On more than a few occasions we have gone to traditional Indigenous leaders to listen to the harm done by Christian missionaries or local pastors. While not making excuses for them, we have tried to create space for remedy. We also created a conference on peacemaking, inviting Southern Cheyenne Peace Chief Lawrence Hart to make a presentation on Cheyenne peacemaking. There was much to learn.

Remember That Humans Are Mostly Good with Some Evil

A common Indian refrain is, "Indian people didn't have a word for sin." It may be more precise to say we do not see ourselves as sinners in the way that some Christians do, with their doctrines asserting original sin. Evil is known among Native Americans, both intrinsic and extrinsic to the human experience, but we do not consider anyone made by Creator to be evil. Even the trickster figures of Indigenous folklore—Coyote, Rabbit, Raven—possess goodness along with their mischief.

What's interesting is that Native Americans remember our failures in our own oral history. Part of the story we shared about the origins of disease and medicine among the Cherokee is that there was a harmony in the beginning that we lost touch with. In the same way, the Iroquois story included cannibalism. If we do not accept responsibility for our wrong actions, how can we change? This worldview implies that we can restore balance by reclaiming what was lost. We have noticed that when people from a Western worldview tell their stories, they have a difficult time admitting their wrongs. Perhaps it is the pressure of American myth that causes people to become the heroes of their own stories. Whatever the cause, Western folks often seem unable to come to grips with the evils in their past.

The divine order of things, according to Indigenous understandings, includes an intricate balance of plants and animals, humans and nature, the Creator and the created. The way in which people lived, the continuation of ceremony, and tribal laws all helped to maintain or restore the balance in the world for which human beings were responsible. Disorder comes when people do not behave correctly with one another or when humans abuse the animal world or other aspects of the whole community of creation.

See Fear as a Catalyst

Through the multitude of human emotions—sadness, anger, and even fear—we are able to recognize our state of being. Such emotions, which can seem negative at first, might actually help us gauge how far out of the Harmony Way we have drifted. Fear can serve as a great catalyst for moving us to practice values such as resolution, generosity, patience, and honesty. Canadian Mohawk Indigenous scholar Taiaiake Alfred tells us, "Bravery is to face challenges with honesty and integrity."

The first challenge in the face of fear is to be honest with ourselves. We need to name our faults, our weaknesses, and our place inside or outside the sacred circle. Only after that can we act according to our values. What if we began to view fear as a signal—something we need to listen to? What if fear is even a catalyst for virtues?

Fear can also result from straightforward danger. During our life together, the two of us have been afraid numerous times. We have been threatened verbally, threatened physically with gunfire, followed on a dark road home by pickup trucks with their lights off, fired from jobs, defriended, had our meetings broken up, lost our home, and lost pregnancies. These and a whole host of other situations have been downright frightening. Being honest with our emotions got us through these horrifying situations. We learned that to live in fear is to live in imbalance. This imbalance affects not only our own lives but those around us as well.

What situations make you fearful? Is your fear founded in a sense of being out of sync with the Harmony Way or in real risk and danger?

Restore Harmony Where Possible

Remember the Cherokee story at the beginning of the chapter, about the people and the animals and the plants? The story asserts a holistic view of relationships. Harmony was broken between human beings, Creator, and the animals through human ingratitude. The ingratitude was expressed in two ways: in not giving thanks and in killing what was not going to be eaten. Both of these are an affront to Creator and creation. Death came by disease into the world through animals (creation). The healing also came through the creation (plants). Humans were restored to the creation and, as a result, to Creator.

After this story is told, the storyteller often makes this point: for every disease spread to humans by animals, there is a plant that can cure it. This involves balance, restoration, and harmony between the Creator and all creation. The story depicts a time of broken harmony. But through the mending of the hoop, all is restored to the way Creator intended it to be. In Cherokee and other Indigenous ways of thinking, restoration must include holistic relationships between Creator, human beings, and the rest of creation.

The story also teaches us to always be grateful for everything we have. The expression of this gratitude means that we only kill what we are going to eat. Dave Soney, an Ojibway elder and dear friend, once told us about a time when he was ten years old and killed a robin just for fun. His mother made him clean it, cook it, and eat it to demonstrate a similar lesson.

Indian people consider gratitude to be extremely important; it's seen as a part of living in harmony. Among our Indigenous people, most morning ceremonies begin with thanksgiving. The custodial relationship we have with the Earth and with all of creation is expressed as gratitude in all we do. If we are not grateful, we cannot live in the Harmony Way, and we become sick people.

In Native American communities, there is no dichotomy between the physical, the emotional, and the spiritual. Traditionally, when a person is physically ill, a reputable healer will go to that person's home so they can get a fuller picture of what is occurring in the sick person's life. The medicine person asks not only about the physical symptoms but also about dreams, feelings, and relationships that have occurred lately in that person's life. In addition, all medicine given to patients is accompanied by prayer.

Living in harmony is not easy at first. In our current colonial lifestyles, imbalance has come to seem normal, but it isn't. We must shed the tentacles of colonial structures and find ourselves again in harmony with all of creation for all our sakes.

Everything on Earth is at its best when seeking peace, harmony, and balance.

Seek harmony.

8

RESPECT

Honoring the Sacred

We must practice our spirituality. Most Native Americans understand the Great Mystery, or Creator, to be an essential part of a harmony-based lifeway. The sacred imbues everything. In fact, we have met only two Native American agnostics. We have never met a Native American atheist. That's not to say they don't exist; it's just to say that a strong Native value that crosses tribes and characterizes much of Native life is a respect for the sacred. We believe that honoring the sacred is part of the journey to Eloheh.

Yet Native American spirituality can be difficult to parse or categorize. Spirituality is so much a part of everyday reality that it's hard to splinter it off as something separate. While thinking in Western terms, we sometimes refer to Native American spirituality as religion. But religion usually refers to a systematized way of believing in and worshipping the divine. In the Indian way of understanding religion, there is no difference between private, public, and other spheres of thought or expression.

Spirituality is inseparable from Native American life and thought. It is woven into the very fabric of Indigenous life. Among Native Americans, spirituality is integral in everything. It's tangible. Whether ceremony or just the way we conduct ourselves daily, the entirety of life is viewed as a sacred, spiritual path. That is why we talk about the Harmony Way as a lifeway, not a philosophy or ethic or even a religion.

We have noticed people from various tribes doing their own traditional version of morning prayers: Keetoowahs who begin the morning with prayer and a type of water ceremony at a river or creek; Kiowas who burn cedar each morning; Washoes who begin the day by washing their face with water, preferably with water from Lake Tahoe; Muskogee people who face the morning sun for their daily prayers.[‡]

These early morning times of prayer serve as a tangible reminder to Indigenous people that each day is sacred. In this way Native American spirituality is expressed tangibly using water, sunlight, smoke, and many other symbols. But these symbols are also wholly integrated in our hearts.

---

‡   We have seen these things through examples, both shown and shared by various elders, throughout our lives.

In this chapter we look at the Eloheh value of honoring the sacred.

Respect the Great Mystery—Even if That Means Being Silent

Our Indigenous people were already spiritual before contact with settlers and missionaries. Most Native Americans believe either in a supreme being in a personal sense or in a life force in a more distant sense.

We understand God to be the Great Mystery: Creator, life force, or unseen power. To use the term *God* as some religions do—to refer to a personal, private deity—does not represent the broad spectrum of understanding among Native Americans. A broader concept of God—such as the Great Mystery—does not exclude the idea of a personal deity but also allows for varying ways of understanding the Mystery. As Great Mystery or Great Spirit, the divine can be both among us and in the present or more distant, like an unseen power. Still, Native Americans are not as likely to discuss their theology in the details and vocabulary to which the West is accustomed. Speaking about Creator on the West's terms is not something many of us want to do.

In fact, as we began to write this book, we were hesitant and concerned about how to do this. How do we put language around the Great Mystery and ceremony that honors Creator, which goes beyond words? When people endlessly try to explain God to other people, they usually show their own hubris. In our Native American view, too much explanation is evidence of a lack of understanding.

Understand That All Creation Is Both Natural and Spiritual

We understand that Creator made the land, and so land is sacred. Human beings are also walking land made by Creator. Our bodies contain the same kinds of salts and other minerals we find in the Earth, and we decompose easily back to Mother Earth. The land itself and humans *as* land are both in need of healing. When Native Americans think of the Harmony Way, they will invariably mention the Earth, land, or creation as part of their spirituality.

As co-sustainers at Eloheh Indigenous Center for Earth Justice, we take our responsibility to the land very seriously. We have ceremony surrounding various events, such as planting and harvesting. If the land is treated badly, we will feel badly. Once again, this relationship is hard to explain in words. But there is very much a sense that we are an extension of the land, not separate from it. This understanding is key to living out Eloheh.

Land is paramount to our understanding of the Harmony Way. Land not only gives identity, but as we mentioned, in many tribal groups a particular land is often a part of the covenant story between the people and Creator. Land is seen as both a gift and a responsibility for caretaking.

Tribal peoples have their own stories of origin, and all involve the land. Among the Keetoowah, the story goes that after a long time of human wandering, Creator spoke to the people and gave them their land boundaries and moral boundaries. Creator gave them the Harmony Way of living, or Eloheh, and even a name, which gave them a covenant to the land and a relationship to Creator. Our people often consider the land and the covenant to be one and the same.

It's often said around Indian Country that without our land, we can't be a people. This concept of land, and its relationship to Native American spirituality, is very different from the understanding of Western immigrant peoples. Native American identity is tied to the land given to us by Creator and includes our relationship to Creator. Descendants of settlers tend to live with a *concept* or a *description* of a place, rather than inhabiting, deeply, the actual land. America itself may be more of an idea, to Western immigrants, than a place. To Native America, this is a place: a land to which we belong.

Be Involved in Ceremonies and Traditions

Our tangible spirituality as Native Americans includes ceremonies and traditions. For instance, each year the Karuk people of northern California have an annual Earth renewal ceremony, in which they take seriously their role as humans to heal the Earth. Ceremony may be associated with personal worship and also practiced communally, such as through Earth renewal ceremonies. Ceremonies that began ages ago, as a way of recreating the seasons or renewing the Earth, have now taken on more personal meanings.

As society has changed and modernity has limited what were once abundant resources to our people, the meaning behind ceremony has broadened. Some Sundances were once related to buffalo hunts, but nowadays Sundance expresses a personal vow or renews various commitments. Today, people Sundance for many reasons, but no one does it for the buffalo hunt. As a Keetoowah, I (Randy) wash my face ceremonially each morning. I do this at the sink, because we do not have a creek or spring on our property, but I render it into ceremony. I pray in a specific ceremonial way while I do it. Times change, but our spirituality, and the tangible ways it is expressed, stays constant.

How might you think about ceremony in your own life? Have you looked into the meaning of symbols in your own ancestry? Is there a group with whom you talk about spiritual things? Could the group come up with a practice that connects you to the land or water—even something small?

Support Those Who Sustain Traditions

Special Native American societies, which come together around common identities and shared spirituality, remain vital parts of honoring the sacred. Such societies have served crucial roles in sustaining proper government and cultivating spirituality. Says our friend and elder Vincent Yellow Old Woman: "We had certain societies, like Sundance, and only those society members would know fully what was going on in those meetings. Our society members also kept that harmony. Even though only they knew what was going on inside their circle, it was okay."

Vincent's statement about the importance of particular groups within a tribal community, such as the Sundance Society, reveals an important truth of the Harmony Way. That is, not every individual person needs to be involved in or knowledgeable about every aspect or ceremony. There are responsibilities to maintaining harmony that only involve certain groups; as long as they do their tasks, it contributes to the overall harmony of the group. In the past, these spiritual ceremonies would draw the *support* of the whole community, but they didn't require the *involvement* of all. Tribal societies would act in a sort of vicarious fashion for all the people.

Such tribal societies still exist in Native America. When these special societies fail to practice the ceremonies, people have trouble finding harmony. Our ways worked for us, and our societies and structure were seen as existing for the good of all the people. Every aspect of our lives had important meaning. Unfortunately, the problems of encroaching modernity continue to destroy Native American structures.

As a family, we have supported Native American ceremonies even when they were not our own. We know that tribal societies and the ceremonies they sustain contribute to the overall Harmony Way.

There are lessons here for all of us. How can we affirm and support those who honor the Great Mystery through a specific ceremony and tradition, even if we ourselves are not called to practice it?

Use Symbols in Everyday Life

Honoring the sacred in our everyday lives can be highly symbolic. The four directions—north, south, east, and west—factor into much of Native American spirituality. Color and meaning vary, according to tribal traditions, but many tribes use four or seven cardinal directions while talking about their spirituality. As a Keetoowah, I (Randy) often pray in seven directions. These include the four cardinal directions, then to the Earth, then to the sky, and then finally for myself.

For some Native American people, wampum belts have come to symbolize harmony. When sewn into belts, wampum—which was used in Native America at one time as currency, and then to mark agreement among different peoples—has come to represent spiritual harmony. Other Native Americans, when asked what important symbol gathers their spiritual attention, first think of the pipe. Many tribes have pipe keepers and pipe ceremonies. The significance of this, as explained to us, is that sacred smoke always goes upward, just like our prayers. The pipe is also associated with truth telling or covenant making between two or more people or groups. For some, a simple symbol such as the pipe serves as the center of a whole life of spiritual harmony.

Other tribes have other central symbolic events, such as the Shoshone Sundance, the Cherokee Stomp Dance, or the Kiowa Gourd Dance. These sacred objects, dances, and songs all serve as symbolic reference to a way of living in balance and in harmony.

These symbols and ceremonies were so important to our Indian people that the US government outlawed them for many years. Christian churches also attempted to remove Native American dances, songs, and ceremonies that symbolically served as a focus and catalyst to encourage the people to continue in the Harmony Way. Missionaries sometimes tried to displace Native ritual with their own traditions. Settlers and their descendants knew these symbols and ceremonies were what gave us meaning as tribal people, so both church and state sought to extinguish them.

When you visit a Native American home, you will often notice baskets on the wall, or Indian blankets draped over a couch, or perhaps pottery on the shelf. These are not simply home decor or a personal aesthetic statement. These symbols give us meaning.

What are the symbols that give meaning to your life?

Respect Elders

We can trust our elders and our traditions to lead us into a good path. The Cherokee story of Grandmother Turtle and the expansion of the world has many teaching points, but primary among them is that we should listen first to those among us who are the oldest and wisest. Their wisdom is based on much reflected experience. We don't have space to tell the full story here, but ask us to tell it to you if someday we have the pleasure of meeting.

Here's a very short version of the Cherokee story: When the Earth was first made, it was covered all over with water except one small island. All creatures lived there in harmony. When the island became crowded, Creator told all the animals and humans that if one of them swam to the bottom of the water and collected a handful of mud, Creator would take that little bit of mud and create a great land out of it. Grandma Turtle volunteered to go, but the rest of the creatures told her she was too old and slow. Duck, Otter, and Beaver all attempted to dive down and bring back a handful of mud, and each one failed. Finally, they agreed that Grandma Turtle could go. She dove down and remained below the surface for a long, long time. Finally, on the seventh day, she surfaced. She was no longer living, but she had retrieved the mud—the mud out of which Creator fashioned Turtle Island.

Grandma Turtle braves danger and sacrifices herself on behalf of the whole community of creation. Indians are not surprised to hear that, in this story, Grandmother Turtle's actions turn out to be those that save the community. She represents the oldest and wisest of the group. They understand that the situation will not improve until the elder is heard and her suggestions are heeded.

Our elders are the repository of wisdom. The elders and their stories, ceremonies, and traditions provide the authority in Native American communities.

We once asked for permission to teach on a reservation in Wisconsin from an eighty-five-year-old tribal elder and spiritual leader. During the course of the conversation, he continuously referred back to his own uncle's teachings. We learned that his uncle had lived to be 111 years old! In passing along his uncle's teachings to us, that elder was offering up wisdom and a worldview that predated all of us and our short lives.

What can you do to learn about the sacred from your elders? How can you place yourself near enough to elders, and sit with them long enough, to encounter their wisdom? What can you do to pass on that wisdom to those younger than you?

The Earth and everything on it are sacred. Respect everyone. Everything is sacred.

Respect the sacred.

PART III

THE INSIDE PATH

9

ACCOUNTABILITY

Remembering That We Are All Related

All creation is connected. Among traditional Native understandings is an interconnectedness between human beings and the rest of creation. We view nature with a deep respect and reverence. We understand that our foundational role as human beings is to maintain and repair harmony, which means we should live in connection with the whole community of creation.

The difference here is between living *on* the Earth and living *with* the Earth. It's between dominating another and honoring a relationship. Humans are entwined with nature and her creatures. In Indigenous communities, the idea of conquering or even overseeing creation is considered aberrant and irresponsible. We believe that well-being, happiness, and harmony only come when we are co-sustainers with individuals, society, and nature. Practices in Native ceremony, of all kinds, come from a deep understanding that all things in the universe are dependent on one another.

We have looked at the key values of harmony and respect, which are foundational for the entire journey to Eloheh. They provide the map of the terrain ahead. In this chapter and the next three, we look at four Indigenous values that help us on an inward journey of sorts. Each is connected to how we relate to others, of course—remember, all creation is connected. But each of these four values, which we'll call the Inside Path— accountability, history, humor, and authenticity—help us take stock of our inner selves and prepare us for the outward journey ahead.

We turn now more directly to the journey and destination of the book: Eloheh. Traditional Cherokee practitioners have told me (Randy) that the origin of Keetoowah understandings of the Harmony Way, or Eloheh, came through a direct covenant with Creator many thousands of years ago. This treasured Cherokee story, like many of the stories we've shared, runs deeper than it is appropriate for me to share here. Indeed, out of utmost respect for our traditional people, who are holding on to the remaining vestiges of our historical beliefs, ways, and culture, we are being careful about what we share and what we don't. Neither of us would ever betray their confidence by revealing too much to disinterested parties.

I consider myself to be a practitioner of traditional ways, and I am a keeper of several sacred ceremonies and traditions. But I am not enrolled in a Cherokee Stomp Dance Ground, nor do I reside in one of the few remaining Cherokee traditional communities. I have been fortunate to become friends with such people, and I will attempt to honor them by sharing enough so that you can learn but not so much as to expose what is private. Thus, in these pages, I will share some generalized Cherokee beliefs. I will do so from what would be considered a well-informed but not expert opinion, and I will do so in the spirit of honoring these ways rather than making them available for others to appropriate or misuse.

You might ask: Why have Edith and I shared anything at all? It was Redbird Smith himself, our most revered holy man, who said, "The fires kept burning are merely emblematic of the greater fire, the greater Light, the Great Spirit. I realize now as never before it is not only for the Cherokee but for all mankind." I think he understood the world was getting smaller, and perhaps more out of control, than ever. To keep our ways of living only to ourselves would be contrary to love and harmony. Although some will disagree with us, I find myself of the same spirit as Redbird Smith, and I pray for the coming generations to walk in a good way.

Some Cherokees refer to the Harmony Way in the English language as *balance*. Others call it simply *the Way*. The Cherokee Harmony Way is called by two names, mostly depending on the locale. Generally, Cherokees in Oklahoma refer to *Eloheh* both as a *way* of living and as a real *place*: where the Harmony Way was practiced in a special way or under special circumstances. Cherokees in North Carolina and the eastern part of the country often use the Cherokee word *Duyukti*, which connotes the English word *righteousness*, to refer to a way of living in harmony. Wherever this way was practiced they tend to call a place of Eloheh.

I have also heard *Eloheh* translated as "the green Earth place," although there seems to be no reason for this translation. The implications of "the green Earth place" would be that Eloheh is about good and right living for the Cherokee. Much of this had to do with hunting and agriculture, growing good crops, and having an ample supply of food.

Regardless of the dialect one chooses, *Eloheh* is used as both a noun and a verb. It is considered to be both a place and a way of living. It means all of life is in balance and harmonious with Creator, and all people and all creation are working together in the most natural and mutually conducive ways.

It is from this understanding that preachers (not the same as preachers in churches) at the Stomp Dance Grounds share with the people how to live. Preachers exhort them to pray, to keep harmonious relationships with nature, and to keep familial, clan, and tribal relationships intact.

Yet *Eloheh* is considered to be even broader in the sense that it can refer to an entire worldview. *Eloheh* contains not only the foundational bearing for Cherokee lifeways but also the very history of the Cherokee people and the lands that they were given to co-sustain, or keep.

This connection was made clear during a US Congressional hearing in 1978. To protect Cherokee lands from being flooded by a reservoir, planned by the Tennessee Valley Authority, artist Jimmie Durham explained:

> Is there a human being who does not revere his homeland, even though he may not return? . . . In our history, we teach that we were created there, which is truer than anthropological truth because it was there that we were given our vision as the Cherokee people. . . . In the language of my people . . . there is a word for land: *Eloheh*. This same word also means history, culture, and religion. We cannot separate our place on Earth from our lives on the Earth, nor from our vision nor our meaning as a people. We are taught from childhood that the animals and even the trees and plants that we share a place with are our brothers and sisters. So when we speak of land, we are not speaking of property, territory, or even a piece of ground upon which our houses sit and our crops are grown. We are speaking of something truly sacred.

The conceptual integration of land, history, religion, and culture into a single thing may be difficult for Western minds to embrace. For Native Americans, this integration is often explained as a visceral knowing, or an understanding, somehow embedded in our DNA. This feeling we have of ourselves as a people—including our histories and cultures being connected to the land—is perhaps the single most glaring difference between a Western worldview and a Native North American worldview. In its simplest reduction: the Earth is our mother and all the creatures on the Earth are our relatives.

The Harmony Way makes room for the kind of living that allows respect for these relationships to exist. It calls us to a deep and abiding accountability to one another, to creatures, and to the Earth. In this chapter, we'll look at what that accountability means.

Seek Reciprocity

Reciprocity is one of the unifying principles of Native American understandings. The idea of reciprocity guides living systems toward balance, promoting a sense of belonging and the truth that all things in the universe are dependent on one another. We all understand how the exchange of oxygen and carbon dioxide between trees and other creatures keeps them both living. So, everything created needs other creatures to stay healthy. The entire Earth and all that dwells in it play a part in the other's existence and well-being.

This principle of reciprocity—a give-and-take in a relationship of balance—is not just some transaction done to advance one's own aims. Traditionally, Native Americans see reciprocity as a natural law of the universe and as crucial for humans to maintain harmony. Therefore, it is the responsibility of human beings to restore harmony on the Earth through interventions such as prayers and ceremonies.

Humans are considered the intermediaries. Simply understood, reciprocity is how the universe maintains its order. Day follows night, spring follows winter, and death follows birth. Both giving and receiving make the circle of harmony and balance continue to turn. When our hearts are right, we can see clearly how to heal ourselves, others, and the Earth. In a Native American worldview, reciprocity is the natural order of the created universe, and it applies to everything.

We can create many practical ways to live in better reciprocity with the Earth. For example, we can try our best not to purchase plastics. There are often alternatives we can choose, such as hemp or wheat. Both these products look and feel very much like plastic, but they can be sustainably sourced and don't require extracting petroleum for the Earth. Hemp is now also being used for flooring, clothes, and many other things. Sometimes seeking reciprocity is as simple as choosing one thing rather than another.

Become a Keeper

We call ourselves "co-sustainers" of our regenerative, agro-ecological farm. A more common word than *co-sustainer* among Native Americans, but one that relies on a similar concept, is *keeper*. In traditional circles, people who have been entrusted and trained to maintain certain sacred objects and ceremonies are called keepers. Those people who are trained in sweat lodge are called sweat lodge keepers. A leader of a pow wow drum is a drum keeper. Keepers are crucial in the work of maintaining harmony. Because of this long-standing tradition, we sometimes use the term *keeper* or *Earth keeper*. We believe that every human being is created as an Earth keeper, or co-sustainer, simply by virtue of being born.

At a micro level, we must ask ourselves: When we disturb the Earth, especially by extraction or pollution, what are we destroying? What are we *not* keeping? The Earth contains, in just one healthy handful of soil, billions of organisms such as protozoa, bacteria, nematodes, and miles of mycelia (fungi). In fact, these are the *real* sustainers in nature: the creatures who keep the soil healthy and assist in such important tasks as retaining water. When we destroy any part of the Earth, such as with herbicides, we are killing the co-sustainers of healthy soil, trees, and the ecosystem.

Several years ago, we changed our organizational nomenclature from titles of office, such as president and secretary, to *co-sustainers* to remind us that our primary role is to cooperate with creation and Creator to maintain and restore a harmonious Earth.

What gifts of the natural world are you able to co-sustain? What has been entrusted to you to maintain and keep?

Express Gratitude in Ceremony

Through expressing gratitude in ceremonies, Native Americans reveal to others and themselves the connection between the Creator, human beings, the Earth, and all of creation. The foundation of the Native ceremony is gratitude.

We have observed hundreds of Native American ceremonies from various tribes over the years, and we are quite certain that there has never been one that lacked the element of gratitude. In many of those ceremonies, gratitude is the entire theme. Most prayers by Native Americans also are full of grateful statements, often beginning with the words "We give thanks."

Giving daily thanks for the gifts in creation has always been the normative way of living for traditional Native peoples. The Six Nations of the Haudenosaunee—that is, the confederation of the Mohawk, Oneida, Onondaga, Cayuga, Seneca, and now Tuscarora, who live in New York state and neighboring Canada—express their thanks by reciting a prayer known as the Thanksgiving Address. This address is spoken at ceremonies, schools, and other community gatherings. I have heard this beautiful prayer formally spoken. The words convey gratitude for fellow human beings, Mother Earth, the moon, stars, sun, water, air, winds, animals, plants, and more. Here is one short excerpt: "With one mind, we turn to honor and thank all the Food Plants we harvest from the garden. Since the beginning of time, grains, vegetables, beans, and berries have helped people survive. Many other living things draw strength from them, too. We gather all the Plant Foods together as one and send them a greeting of thanks."

The totality of the prayer includes almost every aspect of creation. Many years ago, our family adopted this prayer to recite around the Thanksgiving table. Each person reads or narrates a paragraph and passes it to the next person, who reads the next paragraph of gratitude. In this way, at least once a year we remind ourselves of the relationship we have to the whole community of creation by naming all our relatives.

Learn from Creation

Creation is a teacher, and we are the students. Because Native Americans do not view the Earth as a static object but rather as living, we have a framework for viewing our relationship with creation as one of dynamic learning. If you believe that each part of creation is imbued with spirit, it changes everything. What if you became a student in the school of creation?

A Comanche elder, Robert Coffee, once told me (Randy) a story about his early education that reveals this keen understanding by an unschooled Comanche mother. During what would become many visits over a two-year period, I sensed he was particularly interested in letting me, an educated Native person, know that there are two kinds of education. Neither of these types of education is bad, per se, but he wanted to be sure I understood the value of the Indian way of learning things.

When he was small, he told me, a missionary came to his parents' home and urged his mother to send him to school. Robert begged her to allow him to walk to the school the next morning. Finally, she agreed. She packed him a lunch and pointed to the woods to the west. "Come back in time to do your chores," she said. The boy tried to correct his mother. "But the school is to the east." She persisted in pointing west. So he spent the whole day in the woods and came home just before dark. "What did you learn today, son?" his mother asked. "Nothing, Mother. I just sat in the woods all day."

Each day was the same, until about the fourth day, when he answered her differently. "I saw a rabbit outsmart a fox today because he could move back and forth more quickly than that fox. Also, I saw a hawk catch a mouse in a field." He described those dynamics. The reports got longer with each stay in the woods until the boy began to look forward to the next day with great excitement. He found himself listening to the wind sing him songs, and he discovered for himself that everything created has a story to tell.

One morning after several weeks, the mother pointed east. "Only now, son, are you ready to go to school."

Over the years, we have talked about and considered this story many times. Both of us have learned, from this and other stories from elders, that we are all interconnected parts of the whole of creation. We are accountable to our teachers. Everything is part of that circle, and life can only make sense when it remains a circle. When we dissect any part of life as if it were separate from the whole, and when we consider one concern without understanding its relationship to the whole, we fail to see life in its fullness. Then it is no longer a circle and becomes linear, and we lose the relationship of the part to the whole.

In the view of our Comanche elder, the rabbit, the fox, the hawk, and the coyote all become teachers from whom we can learn. They teach because they are part of a living system. Stories are developed based on the traits of the animals. Native Americans draw values, humor, wisdom, dances, and other teachings from the remembrance of these stories and from the observation of and experiences with these animals in their environment.

Redbird, our youngest son, grew up hearing from us frequent stories of Grandmother Turtle. You might remember the Cherokee story we recounted in chapter 8, in which Grandmother Turtle sacrificed herself to save the community of creation. Redbird had heard that story and others throughout his childhood. He also knew that whenever we found a live turtle on the road, we always pulled over, got out, and set it out of harm's way. If we found a dead turtle, we always said a prayer and turned it upside down near an ant bed. The ants would benefit from the turtle's flesh, we'd tell our children. Then, when the turtle shell was clean, we'd use the shell to make a rattle. Those rattles helped us to sing our prayers. In all these ways, Redbird had learned to honor Turtle.

During middle school science class, when he had to watch a turtle being dissected, Redbud vomited. It's not that Redbird had a weak stomach. On many occasions, in fact, he had helped us gut and butcher deer, goats, sheep, and fish. But the turtle held sacred value to him. Our son described what they were doing to the turtle at school as evil. He had experienced a very different way of learning from Turtle than the education system did.

We tried to explain to Redbird the purpose of the dissection, but he had trouble understanding how people could learn anything from the turtle by disrespecting it in this way. Redbird was used to understanding the turtle in a larger context of relationship. Western science had upset our son because it did not make room for the relationship of the turtle to the larger context of Redbird's worldview; instead, it treated the turtle as an object with no context other than the purposes of science. We learned a lesson from our son that day.

Ask Questions of Creation

Traditional Native Americans are always looking for a sign as a means of education. It could be an animal, or a shift in the direction of the wind, or even a rock out of place. In all these situations, the view that creation is a teacher is real and pervasive. Theologically, we could even call this learning dynamic "Creator's first order of discourse." Many religions understand creation to be a gift from God, from which people can learn. In the Native American Harmony Way, Creator *continues* to speak through creation, and creation continues to speak to us.

If Great Mystery speaks through creation, might we imagine not only the statements Creator makes through creation but also the questions we might ask? When we move to a new home, we spend time with the land before making any plans. Sometimes we even lie down on the ground to get a better perspective. We ask the land to speak to us.

Questions arise as we spend time with the land, questions such as: What does the land want? Does it need healing, and if so, where? How can we benefit from the land for our needs without preventing the whole community of creation from meeting their needs too?

On our present and prior farms, we set aside space for our nonhuman relatives to flourish undisturbed. We extended wetlands, left sections of woods intact, and restricted access to certain areas. A farmer friend once said that he bends nature without breaking it. That's close to what we do.

On our farm, we pay attention to the land and the other creatures sharing it. We ceremonially bless the seeds each year at planting time. We celebrate with gratitude the harvest time. In between those ceremonies, we talk to our plants. We touch them gently. We sing to them, and we pray for them, just like they are our relatives—because they are.

Remember that we are all related.

10

HISTORY

Looking Forward by Looking Back

Our Mi'kmaq friend Terry LeBlanc tells a story about his grandfather taking him deep into the woods when Terry was young. As they walked together, his grandfather told him to look twice as much at the scenery behind him as he did at the landscape in front of him. As they made their way forward, his grandfather reminded him to keep looking back. If he did not recognize where he had been, his grandfather said, he would never find his way out of those woods.

This story has become a metaphor for Terry as he speaks about our ancestors. Terry's grandfather taught him, in a literal way, how looking back is an act of looking forward.

Looking back at where we've been is the only way to figure out where we will be going.

The Harmony Way includes a time orientation that emphasizes the past and present rather than the future: where we need to be and when. Our spirit echoes from where we have been, meaning that the past matters.

We have frequently heard Native Americans say of people who operate within the confines of the dominant culture, "They have a clock inside their head." They are describing a person who lives their life in relation to a tighter time schedule than Indians generally do. To understand the natural rhythm of Native Americans, especially those living in traditional communities on the reservations or in many parts of Oklahoma, the tighter time schedule must become less rigid.

Colonialism and modernity have driven everyone to the point that we are unable to escape the clocks inside our heads, which drives us toward a future orientation. In Western modernity, time is viewed as a commodity to be kept, saved, cut, lengthened, and managed. The dominant Western culture savors the present and sails into the future without reflecting on the past.

An early study of the differences between Indigenous and non-Indigenous people concerning time orientation called the Values Project, noted that Indigenous people view time differently from how the Western mind views it. Indigenous people honor past traditions as a way of moving forward. In other words, the present can only be seen as stable when there is a continuity with the past.

On a daily basis, this orientation to the past and present may look a lot like taking life as it comes or, frankly, showing up "late" for events. We call it "Indian Time," but most non-Western people have their own version.

Let's examine what a value placed on the past can do to shape our commitments in the future. We'll also look at the way that an orientation to time might give way to an orientation to place.

Accept the Fluidity between the Past and the Present

In 1917, venerated Keetoowah holy man Redbird Smith spoke of his understanding of religion and the present. "This religion as revealed to me is larger than any man," he said. "It is beyond man's understanding. It shall prevail after I am gone. It is growth like the child—growth eternal. This religion does not teach me to concern myself of the life that shall be after this, but it does teach me to be concerned with what my everyday life should be."

"Concerned with what my everyday life should be": in Smith's view, the present was where his spirituality existed. He had little concern for the future. This value—of life lived with a past-focused and present-focused cosmic orientation—can help us understand how Native American life works on a daily basis.

Native Americans generally do not adjust well to the dominant culture's value of time. While it may seem like a good use of time to people from Western cultures to mark the hours and even the minutes, Native Americans tend to value the organic interactions of place and people.

Prioritize Place over Time

The idea of place is related to a creation-based spirituality. The West has historically placed the emphasis on *time*, with little serious thinking about *place*. In a creation-based or land-based spirituality, place takes on relational aspects that may be neglected by an emphasis on time. To return to our understanding of worldviews: those operating under a Western worldview tend to emphasize time, and those within a Native worldview tend to value place.

Empire replaces *local* place with *universal* place. In a colonized reality, sameness and universal recognition are important. Driving down a commercial strip of fast-food restaurants and big-box stores in one state, you might as well be driving down a commercial strip in any state. Corporate empires train consumers to value sameness and predictability of place. Every place begins to look like every other. This view can be passed down to the next generation.

The new generations of event-oriented people are able to pass down the myth of *pseudo-place*. Land-based, place-oriented peoples are more bound to a local place as a base of identity. When place-oriented people are removed from their place—such as when Native Americans were removed from their homelands—they have great difficulty.

Often, such differing views of time and place mean that people just end up talking past each other. Our orientation toward time also has something to do with how we understand truth. Indigenous scholar Vine Deloria Jr. states that place-oriented people are concerned with truth in their own context, whereas time-oriented people tend to make truth abstract and try to apply it to any situation at any time:

> The structure of their [Native American] religious traditions is taken directly from the world around them, from their relationships with other forms of life. Context is therefore all-important for both practice and the understanding of reality. The places where revelations were experienced were remembered and set aside as locations where, through rituals and ceremonials, the people could once again communicate with the spirits. Thousands of years of occupancy on their lands taught tribal peoples the sacred landscapes for which they were responsible and gradually the structure of ceremonial reality became clear. It was not what people believed to be true that was important but what they experienced as true. Hence revelation was seen as a continuous process of adjustment to the natural surroundings and not as a specific message valid for all times and places.

For Native Americans, the value is on the here and now. We look to the present, in the local place, rather than to some future elsewhere. The future has not happened. This is easily illustrated in ideas concerning "Indian time."

What Indian time means practically is that our events and appointments will begin when everyone eventually shows up. Indian time is regulated by place and experience, not by a clock. One example of this is at Native American pow wows. Often the pow wow starts late because the drum or head man or head female dancer or perhaps the arena director has shown up late. It begins only when everyone gets there.

Indian time is a value that goes far beyond just being late, which is how it might look to someone with a clock inside their head. You might be "late" because you were in an important conversation with a friend, or were caring for a child who will not be rushed, or were stopping to help someone who needed assistance. None of these things should be interrupted by some false construct of time.

I (Randy) was once scheduled to speak at a church in Oklahoma that had a reputation for starting on Indian time. The official start time was 10:30 a.m., so we knew better than to come early. We showed up right at 10:30 a.m., just in case, but we were the first ones there. By the time they opened the doors, it was 11:10 a.m., and the service began about twenty minutes after that.

I finally began speaking just before noon. It was 12:30 p.m. when I finished. Several families had come in at various times during my talk. After I had finished, the pastor kindly asked me to give my talk again because not everyone had been there to hear it. That is real Indian time! While Indian time may sound like a small cultural marker, it's not. It embodies the way we approach life: with an eye toward attending to the important things even if it means ignoring the clock.

Are there ways you let a future orientation dominate your life? Does a busy schedule ever rob you of the things that are important to you? If so, what might you do to prioritize those values over your commitment to the clock?

Determine the Future by Looking to the Past

When we pass our traditions down to the next generation, we are passing down the presence of all our ancestors who came before us. Those songs and stories and teachings are not just from us but from those who came before us. Our ceremonies connect us to our ancestors because we know they once stood where we now stand, using the same traditions.

I (Edith) bead Indian jewelry. My mother also did great Indian beadwork. Often when I am beading, I find my thoughts drifting to my mother, especially when I look at my hands. I think about what she would do with a color or a stitch, or how she looked for patterns or asked my dad what he thought. Then I ask Randy the same questions. In some ways, my mother is there with me during that practice. Randy's mom loved nature, especially birds and flowers. When he sees exceptionally beautiful birds or flowers, his mother always comes to mind. "My mom would love this one," he often says to me when he sees a hummingbird or a robin or a pretty flower. Our ancestors are always present to lead us into the future.

When sharing stories, Native American elders often drift freely between current and past events. They may begin a story by saying something like "A long time ago . . . ," but if you listen carefully, you'll notice that the behavior or problem they are addressing is likely a current one. Indigenous learning comes through reflected experience. We learn about how to live now by examining what has happened in our history.

We depend on our stories, our ceremonies, and other traditions to guide us to a good future. Often that future is best expressed through exploring things from the past. We mine our past for those gems that are our payment for the future. That is why our stories and other past concerns are so very important. Without our past, we cannot be a people in the future.

Think about what you have carried forward from your parents, grandparents, or caregivers. What practices, ideas, or lifeways rooted in the past are you keeping alive?

Remember That Our Present Reality Will Affect Future Generations

A Native friend once told us that our spirit echoes from where we have been and follows us to where we are going. As we live in our present, we need to remember that the spirit of the present will follow us into the future.

Only when we view the importance of the past as critical to the way we live the present can we project what might be our future. It is not as though Native Americans don't think about the future. We have an attitude that all things will eventually unfold in their time. As we understand it, this is not a statement of a predetermined cause but rather one that reveals the importance of living in the moment.

In the same way that there is a relationship between Native American views of the past and the present, there is a relationship between the present and the future. One teaching among many tribes is that what we do today will affect the next seven generations. This seven-generations thinking is a widely held warning among Native Americans when considering the relationship between our present decisions and the lives of those in the future. The future is important, but it can only be lived well by regarding our past.

Look forward by looking back.

11

HUMOR

Laughing at Ourselves

Once, when we were hanging around Arizona with a bunch of Navajo people, they began to talk about a baby's first laugh. They were warning the person holding the baby to be careful because the baby had not laughed yet. They told the person, "If you make the baby laugh, you are responsible for sponsoring the first laugh ceremony." The idea, as we understood it, was that when the baby has its first laugh, it becomes a real person. That is truly something to celebrate! We think the Navajo have it right: laughing, among all the other ways it affects us, makes us real human beings.

Non-Indians are often surprised when they discover the sense of humor that permeates much of Native America. In the same way they created the image of the "Indian warrior," Hollywood created the image of the stoic Indian: silent, humorless, and grim.

When Native Americans describe themselves and their cultures, they often mention humor. Indigenous cultures are rife with stories of tricksters and clowns, funny ways of describing daily events, jokes about ourselves and jabs at others. Native elders can often be heard telling young people to enjoy themselves and have fun, because they know that laughter and playfulness are an important part of life's balance.

In fact, humor is considered sacred among many Native groups. "Most Native American sacred traditions have a common belief that humor is a necessary part of the sacred," write Peggy V. Beck and her coauthors in *The Sacred: Ways of Knowledge, Sources of Life*, which help readers understand how Native Americans view the world. "Human beings are often weak—we are not gods: our weaknesses lead us to do foolish things. . . . Too much power, too much seriousness, were to be feared for they too could 'unbalance' life in the community and environment. We are taught by the clown, among others, not to take ourselves too seriously. This means, not to make ourselves too important. We are not *that* indispensable."

It may seem to outsiders that our humor is often self-deprecating or that we are particularly tough on each other. But our humor stems from a grounded awareness of human frailty. Indian humor serves the function of reminding us that we are just human beings. Being human is a good thing. Our stories of tricksters, with their grandiose plans and plots, remind us that to try to be something more than human—more than what we are created to be—is pure foolishness.

Humor is culturally situated, and what makes one person laugh might make another person wince. No matter the variety of humor, though, we know that laughter and light-heartedness are essential elements of the Harmony Way. Humor shifts our attention, releases tension, and restores balance. Humor is sacred and necessary.

Make Humor Part of the Balance

Among our Native American communities, we have found that plenty of people are willing to use humor to point out our humanity and potential imbalance. Our humor is often self-deprecating and sometimes even brutal. Indians often laugh at our unfortunate circumstances, which can be disorienting for outsiders. But self-deprecating humor brings us back in balance. One tribe we know of even has a teasing clan.

We mentioned earlier that we often balance out our sweat lodge ceremony with humor when things get too serious for too long. Other ceremonies have humor built into them, too, although we may be losing some of this to modernity. Just a few generations ago, many pow wows had clowns who kept people laughing. Now the emcee's job is to keep people laughing.

The late Bryan Bright Cloud was a master at Indian humor as a pow wow emcee. Often his jokes were directed at the White people attending the pow wow. This is a bit edgy. But in Indian Country, humor is just what you get. They say if you aren't being teased, nobody likes you.

Bryan's jokes from the microphone included this one, aimed at White attendees: "Be sure you stop by the Indian casino down the road before you go home tonight. They are looking forward to your reparation money."

And here's another: "This announcement is for all the White people attending the pow wow. We're glad you're here, and we have a special gift for you. Please come up and get your free Indian pills. Within an hour, you will notice a significant decrease in your desire to steal Indian land, horde things for yourself, and take yourself so seriously."

Humor helps us achieve balance. When things get too serious, a lighthearted comment, joke, or witty aside can help us find our center.

Laugh at What Can Kill You—Before It Does

Humor can also serve as a survival strategy of sorts—a way to defy and distract. Most Native American sacred teachings and practices contain humor. Often our stories contain a trickster-hero such as Coyote, Raven, or Rabbit. Trickers are both wise and foolish. They can be heroic and afraid. One of the aims of the tricksters is to remind us, like the first laugh ceremony does, that we are human.

The mythical figures in our stories are allowed to ask questions and act in ways that we are not. Tricksters can do the things that we only dream of doing. They are also there just to make us laugh. In *The Sacred*, Beck and her coauthors refer to "sacred clowns." The authors remind us that, amid the seriousness of life, sacred clowns help us keep life in balance:

> Fundamentally, the sacred clowns portray a Path of Life with all its pitfalls, sorrows, laughter, mystery and playful obscenity. They dramatize the powerful relationships of love, the possibility of catastrophe; the sorrow of separation and death; the emerging consciousness of human beings entering into life—entering this world as ordinary beings with non-ordinary potential. They show the dark side; they show the light side; they show us that life is hard; and they show us how we can make it easier. If death takes everything away when it robs an individual of life, then the Clowns must be able to combat death in mock battle and wrestle life back again.

In some ways, the clowns of Native American myth are actually therapists in disguise. The clowns know that sometimes people need to laugh at their awful situations in order to keep them in perspective.

Maybe there is a difference between humor and foolishness. But many Native Americans view the dominant culture as being far out of balance in this regard. "Why do they take themselves so seriously?" is a common question about White people that you'll hear in Indian Country.

Perhaps our health and well-being are tied to our ability to laugh at ourselves. Laughter is connected to creativity, and humor can help us see the world in surprising ways. The journey to Eloheh has to include the kind of sacred humor that enlivens our spirits. Otherwise, it won't be sustainable.

So why not laugh at what could kill you—before it does?

One of our best friends, the late Richard Twiss, was extremely adept at Indian humor. Besides being an incredible speaker, Richard, who was Sicangu Lakota Oyate, could hold a crowd's attention like no other. He was the author of several books, including *Rescuing the Gospel from the Cowboys*. In lectures, he'd be delivering incredibly serious subject matter—colonialism's erasure of Native culture, the genocide of Native people—and he would use humor in an incredibly sophisticated way to make his point. We used to say that Richard would get audiences laughing so much that they didn't realize it was the knife in their ribs that was tickling them.

Richard always had a joke, and he was particularly good at keeping the people around him humble with his humor. Once at an event, he held up one of my (Randy's) books and told everyone that they all should read it. Then he announced, "As a one-time special, today only, Randy is giving away a free box of Crayolas to go along with the book."

That kind of humor goes both ways in Indian Country. At an event in Calgary, Alberta, that our family was attending, Richard greeted us and began to tease our youngest son,

Redbird, whom, as he did to all our children, he referred to as his nephew (or niece, in the case of our daughters). Richard went on to tell Redbird, "This is the place where all the smartie-pants Indians are."

"Then what are you doing here?" Redbird deadpanned. That may be the only time we ever saw Richard unable to respond with a comeback.

Humor often uncovers truths that might otherwise remain unspoken. Native Americans and other people who have been at the mercy of settlers often found humor to be a subversive way to hold onto their identity and values. Jokes and other things that make us smile also serve as containers for our worldview. They can remind us who we are. They remind us to be humble.

Humor reminds us that we are just human beings.

Laugh at yourself.

12

AUTHENTICITY

Speaking from Your Heart

There's a story told on the Wind River Indian Reservation about the noteworthy Shoshone Chief Washakie, who lived through most of the nineteenth century. Washakie was being honored by the president of the United States with a silver saddle. The president's aides had accompanied the gift all the way to Wyoming, and journalists were there, ready to report the old chief's reaction.

After the gift was given, Washakie said nothing. One of the envoys asked Washakie to comment. Still, Washakie stood in solemn silence. Again, the men from Washington pressed the chief for a response. "Don't you want to send a message back to the Great White Father in Washington,

DC?" one of them asked. Yet Washakie never moved his lips.

Members of the press and government officials alike were indignant. How dare this old Indian slight the president in this way?

One more time they asked Washakie for a response. Finally, the uncomfortable silence was broken. This time Chief Washakie moved slowly to the center of the platform. He opened his mouth to say just these few words: "The White man thinks with his mind, and he has many words to describe his thoughts. The Indian thinks with his heart, and the heart has no words."

In understanding the Harmony Way, we need to talk about how we speak—and how we don't. We need to consider the differences in how we all use words. For many Indigenous people, there is a sort of primal power in our words and especially in our oral traditions. The journey to Eloheh includes thinking carefully about our words and what they reveal. It means learning to speak from the heart.

Learn When to Speak Certain Words—and When Not To

Hearing truth, to traditional Native people, is about hearing the words from a person's heart.

In Indian Country, a person must make oneself vulnerable to be heard. A person's words, along with their heart, are judged at that time by the community. If the community who witnessed those words is absent later, they will be considered "out of context" when others examine those words. Words taken out of context are not important because they don't impart the same understanding they did when they were given.

Certain words are seen as more sacred and more powerful than others among Native Americans. One example among some tribes is the use of names for Creator. In some traditions, one name that represents Creator is only to be spoken under particular circumstances. Other names for the Creator may be freely spoken.

While attending a Kiowa funeral, we were told that we could speak the deceased person's name for three days only. After that, we would be in danger of calling that person's spirit back. Since that time, we have observed similar traditions among other tribes.

Words carry incredible power, and Native people know this. Words can create reality, and so we need to choose them carefully. Knowing when not to use certain words is very important.

Understand the Reasons for Mistrust of Words

Some of us have reasons, rooted in history, to mistrust the words—especially the written words—of others. *Smoke Signals* was the first major film to be written, directed, produced, and acted in primarily by Indians. In this movie, Victor, the young Indian protagonist, is trying to convince his mother that he will keep his word and follow through on something he has promised. He asks her whether she wants him to sign a paper. "No way!" his mother replies. "You know how Indians feel about signing papers!"

Native Americans mistrust the words of treaties—and well we should. That fact has as much to do with the form of a written document as it does with the content. Our history is littered with broken treaties and official-looking documents that made certain promises and then ended up harming us. Now governmental bureaucracy accomplished the same purpose.

We have heard Native elders say, "I don't like talking on the phone because I can't see the person's heart who I'm talking to." There is a general mistrust among our people, especially our traditional people, of any form of communication except face-to-face conversation. The broken treaties only serve to substantiate the mistrust in all forms except face-to-face encounters.

Perhaps it's harder to speak mistruths to someone when you are speaking to them in person. Trust is created in the context of conversation, over time. Think about the reasons you have to trust—or mistrust—others' words. Consider why certain groups of people might be less trusting of words—especially official ones—than others. In what ways does the past form our level of trust or mistrust?

Pass Down Traditions Orally

There are sacred figures among many of our tribes—historic and mythical figures who arrive on the scene and deliver transformative messages. They came to our people and redirected or reinforced our values, giving us the ability to endure great periods of hardship or leading us to the right path.

The traditions of our Indigenous people are not trends or fads. They have been passed down orally for hundreds, thousands, and sometimes tens of thousands of years.[§] Because stories, ceremonies, and objects often accompany these traditions—including places; natural features such as the sun, moon, and stars; and certain species of animals, trees, and insects—they have remained fairly stable. The continued passing down of stories and traditions seems to help to ensure a return to or maintenance of the Harmony Way.

The original peace and harmony that Indigenous people have among themselves works until someone divides the community. The dilemma then is: How do people restore their dignity and unity when it has been lost? How do we mend the hoop?

Indian people restore their dignity by returning to their stories, which have been passed down orally from one generation to the next. What types of stories have been passed down to you? What stories are you passing on to the next generation?

[§] Our Cherokee Cedar Fire ceremony is an example of a traditional ceremony that traveled with our people from a time before we came to the Great Smoky Mountains and before we were given our name by the Creator. Even most conservative estimates would affirm this point in time to be over 10,000 years ago. New forensic science is beginning to point to a 40,000-year-plus point of American entry for Native Americans, with some estimates as high as 200,000 years ago.

Listen to the World around You

Native American communication is generally done quietly, discreetly, and respectfully. In our experience, Indians can also get loud, expressive, and even boisterous. We state this to avoid the danger of stereotyping Native Americans as stoic. Under many circumstances, nothing could be further from the truth.

With all that said, general observations are helpful here. Native people do often have a certain demeanor while listening to others in instructive situations. Because we are primarily an oral culture, our Native people tend to have highly refined listening skills. Listening is the key to understanding others. Listening is perhaps the greatest compliment one person can pay to another. By listening we are giving dignity and respect to others. We are giving them an immense gift.

Traditionally, we have been taught to listen in all circumstances. When you are in the woods, it is not just your vision that becomes important but also your listening skills. For example, a river that is shallow has a bubbling sound and is louder than the quiet, sleepy sound of a deep river. Perhaps people are the same? A Machupta/Maidu elder once told us how to listen to the sound of birds while looking for herbal medicines in the woods. According to the elder, the sound of certain birds will lead you to the medicine you are seeking.

In order to be a culture that values both oral tradition and the world around us, Native Americans have learned to be good listeners. How might you begin to listen to the whole community of creation that surrounds you?

Speak Vulnerably—Which Takes Courage

In 2018, we were invited to an interfaith gathering. It was a group of leaders from religious communities all over Oregon. The first night, everyone started introducing themselves. Mostly people talked about what church, synagogue, temple, mosque, or denomination they represented, including what position they held and what wonderful things they were doing. We walked away from that night thinking to ourselves that we were glad that we didn't belong to any formal religion or denomination. It seemed to us that some were trying to outdo each other. Who was the most important? Who was doing the most impressive things? We wondered together whether any of them understood what it means to speak from the heart.

The next morning was more of the same but in smaller groups. The assignment was to share from the heart, and so when it was our turn, we shared deeply about the struggles we faced in our leadership and the difficulties at hand. We think we made some of the other people uncomfortable with the depth of our sharing because some just looked down at their hands the whole time.

Later, during a break, we decided to go to the leaders and tell them what we had just experienced. This exercise was clearly designed to invite participants to speak from the heart, but everyone appeared to be speaking entirely from the head. The leaders brought up the issue to the group, and something wonderful began to happen. From that point forward, people began sharing from their hearts in a more personal manner. It was as if all they needed was permission.

What would it look like to give yourself—and others— permission to speak from the heart? When we speak from the heart, we get to know each other in a more personal way. We become vulnerable. It's difficult to be vulnerable. If you've ever been in a setting like the one we've just described, in which people are trying to impress each other, you know it takes courage to speak authentically and vulnerably. But we need to be vulnerable if we are ever going to get to know each other on a level past superficiality. Vulnerability is a way to share our deepest sense of humanity. Vulnerability, like laughter, makes us human. And being human is perhaps our deepest spirituality.

We have heard it said that you can only move as a group at the speed of trust. We prefer to say that we can all move together at the speed of courage. The courage to be vulnerable.

Speak from your heart.

PART IV

THE OUTSIDE PATH

13

EQUALITY

Listening to Everyone

In the old days, every Cherokee village was built near a river or a creek. All the houses were built just above the floodplain. The spring floods would eventually subside, and those huge fields were then naturally fertilized with silt and ready to be planted with corn, beans, squash, and other good foods.

In the middle of the floodplain would stand a huge mound. The mound was commensurate with the size of the village, which was commensurate with the amount of food that could be grown. On top of the large mound sat a council house, large enough to accommodate meetings for every person in the village at once.

When the British first started dealing with the Chero-kees, they became very frustrated. They were used to kings and hierarchies that made absolute decisions with a word. The Cherokees had no such hierarchies or kings. Emissar-ies from Great Britain would say things of the Cherokees like, "They take three or four days just to make a simple decision!" and, "Every person in the village must have a say before reaching a decision." They even called the Cherokee a "petticoat government," because the women had equal say. This way of making decisions was incomprehensible to the British, but it demonstrates a key value of Keetoowah equality.

We turn now toward the final four values. You might think of these four as composing the "outside path" of Elo-heh. Equality, community, balance, and generosity turn us toward each other. The Indigenous value we look at in this chapter—equality—includes practices such as consensus building, cooperation, and recognition of the basic dignity of others. Equality is, in its most basic form, everyone get-ting a say.

Work Cooperatively

Sometimes you see things most clearly by looking at their opposite. The value of equality is perhaps most easily observ-able when you think about what it is *not*. Words such as *individualism, patriarchy, hypermasculinity, independence, selfishness*: these attributes press in the opposite direction from equality. I once asked a class composed mostly of students from other countries what words best described Americans to them. Along with the list above, a number of them answered, "John Wayne." When you think about John Wayne and what he represents in terms of extreme individualism and competition in the majority American culture, you could say he is the embodiment of the American myth.

A cooperative culture, as opposed to a more competitive culture, tends to show values such as respect, tolerance, a keen understanding of diversity and consensus. These subsidiary values are related to community and serve to make possible the uniqueness of Native American community.

Perhaps the overriding value to be found here is respect. Although we don't always agree with the things others do, we must still have respect for their choices. We do not have to practice others' beliefs, but we must respect them.

Consider Consensus

The ability to listen is key to Native American community—and community of any kind. We saw the importance of listening in chapter 12.

Our experience with the American system, in a 51 percent / 49 percent type of vote, means one group overpowers the other. It smacks of the force and violence typical of colonial patterns. How can community be built when half the people disagree?

There is a good understanding in Indigenous communities of the interaction between unity and diversity. Everyone's voice is important because consensus is foundational in the process. In consensus, everyone has a voice, and everyone has a different role to play in the consensus-making process. The result is respect for diversity and strength in unity. Individual autonomy is exercised and respected in the group. But in the end, the group is more important than one's individual autonomy.

Our church in Nevada, Eagle Valley Church, operated on a consensus model, and things went very well. The people who were most respected in the community always seemed to draw in others and convince others to go along with the decision. Our Eloheh board operates on a consensus basis as well. We find this the easiest model in which to operate where everyone is respected and we can move together in unity. It may take longer to make decisions, but the results are worth the effort.

Respect the Dignity of Other Human Beings

We've already looked at respect as a foundational value on the journey to Eloheh. Respect is of utmost importance when we seek to live out the value of equality.

As we mentioned in chapter 5, Anadarko, Oklahoma, has a problem in that it has many unemployed and houseless people. To go deeper into that story, when we saw the problem of houselessness in Anadarko, we had to think of a way to give people whose dignity had already been assailed a way to feel respected. We wanted to recognize their inherent human dignity and to honor their own agency and empowerment. As mentioned, our center already handed out food vouchers and, on inclement-weather nights, motel vouchers. But how could we do more to respect the dignity of unhoused people?

We had the idea—which should be anything but novel—to ask them: What do you need? What do you want? What do you know about your situation and how to improve it that we don't? We gathered them together and simply asked the questions. After they had processed those questions for a while, we saw what they were really asking for was a place to shower and a place to do their laundry. That's why we built such a place within the gym. We had a long way to go, but we were learning to respect the dignity of even those society had decided were disposable.

Tolerate and Respect Dissent

In order to maintain harmony, Native Americans are deliberately tolerant, showing deference to other viewpoints, especially in matters of religious concern. Native Americans embrace the sovereignty of religious beliefs, whether among individuals, families, tribes, or nations.

The value placed on dissent can be seen in the story of Grandmother Turtle that we shared in chapter 8. On three occasions Grandmother Turtle volunteered to dive for the mud, only to be squelched by the decision of the group. She was finally able to act on her idea only when the group could not come up with a better idea for a volunteer.

The way Cherokee people went to war is another example that favors the autonomy of the individual even within the context of the group. The Keetoowah originally had a number of major villages, or "fires," as they are called. Very rarely, if ever, did all those villages ever decide unanimously to go to war. Instead, only certain villages would decide to go to war, and this was usually a result of local concerns, such as a dispute over rights to hunting grounds. The idea of a national war was virtually unknown to early Cherokees or other tribes, as far as we can tell.

Neighboring villages often did assist one another in warring efforts. Still, even if a village did decide to go to war, not every warrior in the village had to participate. Each warrior would decide for themselves, and their autonomy was respected. Then, even if a warrior decided to join the war party but had second thoughts along the way, their autonomy was completely respected, and they could return home in dignity. In this example the importance of the group decision is respected as well as the autonomy of the individual. For community to be valued so highly, respect through consensus making of some sort must be key.

Among Native Americans, it is generally understood that no one should tell another what they must believe. Any type of coercion is seen as breaking the Harmony Way.

Make Decisions by Consulting Your Heart and Your Community

In dominant American culture, people often make decisions based on objective factors. Just think about the guidance you've heard for how to make a decision: *Make a list of pros and cons. Which decision would make financial sense? What are your goals, and how will you accomplish them?* Generally, a Western worldview understands feelings as among the least important criteria.

Among Native Americans, how one *feels* about a decision is paramount. Indians are often known to think with their hearts and minds. In other words, a decision must not only be reasonable; it must feel right. In fact, we have seen many decisions made by Native Americans in which how a person—or community—feels about a decision overrides simple reason.

We believe a good mind is linked to a good heart. When we fail to consult the heart on matters of importance, disharmony is sure to follow. Listening to everyone, the baseline guidance for this value of equality, also means listening to yourself.

Indigenous decision-making is also much more communal than the individualistic approach of dominant American culture is. Am I acting in my own best interest or in the best interest of the people? It is true that sometimes these two interests are aligned. But when they are not, and when people forgo their own interests for the sake of others, those sacrifices are usually honored by the community.

What decisions lie ahead of you? How might you consult your community? What might it look like to think not with your mind but with your heart?

Diversity Gives Strength and Balance to Life

Many Native Americans speak of the four cardinal directions in terms of representing the gifts of different ethnic groups. For example, we have heard some people say the north represents the European tribes, and its gift is technology. They say the diversity of human beings makes the whole human race stronger. Our Indian people understand that the principle of diversity brings strength and balanced unity. This value of diversity is simply understood among Indigenous peoples.

Our Native American people know that community is based on cooperative values, or communality. Each person, clan, and society has a different role to play in promoting strength through diversity. When everyone is cooperating by working within this shared value, there is harmony.

Listen to everyone.

14

COMMUNITY

Increasing Friendships

When I (Randy) moved to western Oklahoma, I had no relatives there. Libby, the Kiowa woman who would become my adopted mother, had lost a son to cancer the year prior, and Creator had shown her that another son would be coming. I was adopted by her family, and later by another family, as a son. I was adopted as a nephew by a Kiowa/Comanche couple and as a brother by a Cheyenne family. I also have an adopted elder brother and an Arapaho brother. The formal adoption process among Native Americans is an extension of a deep and profound sense of community.

Many Native tribes have such "making a relative" ceremonies. The adoption ceremonies are still in place, not as much anymore because of necessity but out of hospitality. No one should be alone in the Indian community. Adoption is a formal way to welcome people with no relatives into the community.

We are remarkably related to everyone and everything. This truth, which we have written of throughout this book, has major implications for how we understand family, friendship, and community. If we are all kin, that truth might be sufficient to transform our lives.

Much has been written about the epidemic of loneliness in Western cultures. In May 2023, US Surgeon General Dr. Vivek Murthy raised alarm about high rates of alienation and loneliness, suggesting that it had reached the level of a public health crisis. Both mental and physical health are related to social connection, and, according to the advisory released by Murthy's office, lacking social connection "can increase the risk of premature death as much as smoking 15 cigarettes a day." A 2022 study found that "when people were asked how close they felt to others emotionally, only 39 percent of adults in the U.S. said they felt very connected to others." The report argues that lack of social connection, alienation, and loneliness represent "an urgent public health concern."

Indigenous people had to rely on each other just to survive the arrival of the settlers and the era of colonization. It made sense for families to create extended relationships among themselves and among other tribes. A sense of kinship often expands in crisis, and Indigenous tribes were facing crisis after crisis after crisis.

Yet that sense of kinship preexisted contact with settlers. It was written into the Native worldview before the time of testing. The Harmony Way circle, symbolizing the idea that we are all connected, had long shaped Native thinking about community. Native Americans believe that we are all made by the same Creator, which makes us relatives—and this is not merely symbolic. We see ourselves as truly related to all creation. A deep bond of trust is found within Native American families and extended relatives, and that bond is sacred.

Again, this concept of making relatives goes beyond survival mode, and it preexisted the colonial period. It is integrated into the values of sharing and hospitality. In other words, it is based not just on reciprocity but on a true sense of generosity. It is also based on the sense of being connected or related to all things.

In this chapter we'll look in a bit more depth at the Indigenous value of community.

Expand Your Sense of Who Belongs

Growing up, we both had people in and out of our homes constantly. That was the normal we knew. Some of the people who would stop by and stay with us were blood related, and some were not. But they were our community, people on whom we could rely. Even though I (Edith) sometimes felt lonely as a child and longed for friends, I was surrounded by community, family, and networks of extended kin. I really did not know what loneliness meant until I left for college and was separated from my community.

When we got married and started our own family, we found ourselves not so alone. Randy knew so many people, and his Indian adoptions were very real. Although I didn't really know these people at first, Libby, Randy's adopted Kiowa mom, took me aside and taught me many things about living in relationship and community. For instance, Libby showed me how to support Randy as he was dancing as a new member of the Tai Pai Society, one of the Kiowa Gourd Dance societies.

I saw Libby as a woman with wisdom: someone who knew what needed to be done in the proper way things should be done. I learned so much from her. It was easy to listen to her as she told stories about her boarding-school days and her life as a child and young adult. She became very much a mother to me, instructing me in the way of traditional things. Even though she was not a blood relative, I felt loved and cared for by her.

As we have traveled all over Canada and the United States, we have come across so many different people who have a special place in our lives. They have become a real part of our family. Although they did not come from the same parents as us, they became family, and we are especially related.

Who composes your network of kin? What does your community look like? How might you expand your notion of who belongs to your family?

Reject Individualism

Embracing community often requires rejecting individualism. There exists a palpable sense of community among Native Americans, and it isn't accidental. Sometimes the community can be seen as protective and guarding, and sometimes it is inviting and expanding. Whether protective or inviting, it is observable and almost never ambivalent. When one is far from tribe and homeland, the generic term "Native American" takes on new meaning. In urban settings, where Native Americans are the extreme minority population, we have observed instant friendships extended to other Natives who were traditionally tribal enemies.

As an educator, I (Randy) have noticed the difficulty Native American students have in succeeding without a strong Native community behind them and supporting them. That support might look like a cohort model or peer tutoring or Native student support group. The individual drive to succeed is just not as self-propelling among Native American students as it tends to be among their Euro-American classmates. The Indian students need to feel they are a part of a larger purpose. Just getting ahead, for their own individual sake, doesn't tend to motivate them. Native students tend to devalue personal achievement and competitiveness, in part because they view it as breaking harmony.

This type of individualism creates an imbalance, and Native students tend to intuit that truth. Extreme individualism, which is often rewarded by Western cultures, will eventually lead Indian people to an identity crisis. The family structure, the community, doesn't want you to go too far to tip the scale, so you keep that balance. In other words, you don't want to go too far from where you come from. The implication is that when you wander too far from where you come from, you forget who you are. Staying close to family and community—or, we would add, even friends who share the same values—aids in ensuring that Native Americans will remain in harmony.

Who makes up your community? Your extended family? Your friends?

Value Women as Sacred

Another important value related to community among Native Americans is the importance of women. This is especially true in matrilineal societies, but it can also be seen in more patrilineal Native American tribal groups. In the past men, in most traditional societies, were the ones who needed to prove themselves, whether through wisdom in leadership, hunting skills and accompanying generosity, prowess as a warrior, participation in societies (religious, medicine, or other societies), and other attributes. Men were often the ones who had a lesser a priori status in traditional societies.

Our friend Fern Cloud, speaking from a traditionally oriented Dakota perspective, draws a clear distinction in the role of women and men by saying that women have the power to create life through birth. "It's no coincidence that White Buffalo Calf Woman was the messenger and Mary was a woman," she told us, comparing the sacredness of

Mary, the mother of Jesus, and White Buffalo Calf Woman, the most sacred messenger of the Dakota, who imparted the Dakota virtues and ceremonies. "Women are sacred and have a lot of respect because they have been given the gift to create." She is implying that both White Buffalo Calf Woman and Mary were chosen by Creator to give birth to a way of life. In Native thinking, by virtue of the giftedness of their bodies, women carry the power of giving birth, and all women are uniquely sacred.

See Children as Our Teachers

When you go to an Indian home, you see how they love their children. We might consider their love for their children to be a hallmark of the Harmony Way.

Of course, Native Americans aren't the only ones who love their children. What is uniquely Native American is how this love for children is related to harmony.

Children have a way of sensitizing us to our faults. Coming back into a life of compassion, or back in the circle, is a lesson easily taught by our children. Because Native Americans are ready for anything in life to be a vehicle from which Creator teaches, we are able to see children as teachers. We once heard a Lakota teacher say that the reason children are sacred to them is that they were with the Creator before their birth. He used a similar rationale to explain why he thought elders were sacred: because they are nearing the end of their lives and they drift in and out of a state that will place them next to God.

It is also notable that many extended family members and others in the community have a role in raising the children. The adage "It takes a village to raise a child" is also true among us. We mentioned our friend Richard Twiss earlier. He was essentially an uncle to our children. He would sometimes hear from us about something going on with one of our children. Unknown to us, he would call them on the phone and give them a chance to share with him, in his uncle role. We found out these things from our children only after our dear friend's death.

We once heard Chief Lawrence Hart, a Southern Cheyenne peace chief, talk about recognizing the uniqueness of each child in the tribe. He spoke about how the elders, particularly the women elders, would closely observe the children of that tribe to discover the unique giftedness bestowed on them by Creator. For example, if one child was particularly generous in sharing with the other children, they would consider that an attribute of leadership. They knew that, during tough times, that person would direct the tribe toward resources for the good of the group and not just themselves. Also, children who had frequent strange dreams and spiritual encounters might be taken into apprenticeships with healers and medicine people to develop their giftedness.

Respect Elders

One of the cardinal rules in Indian Country is to never interrupt an elder when they are speaking. We have learned to emphasize this point to Euro-Americans while trying to sensitize them to Native American culture. Unless they are warned—and sometimes even when they have been warned—White people, to the horror of the Natives present, will sometimes freely start talking right in the middle of an elder's speech. This exemplifies a huge difference between Native American values concerning elders and dominant American cultural values.

For Native Americans, though, this deference to our elders go beyond rules about interruptions. We were taught to give seats to elders first, to assist elders by carrying things for them or opening doors, to never send an elder away from a meal without a plate of food to take home, and to always bring a gift when visiting an elder. In potlucks or any community meal, elders always go first or are served first.

Elders are the most important members of the Indian community. They are valued and respected without hesitation for the vital role they play.

Think about the interactions you have with elders in your family and community. What does respect for them look like in your everyday life? How can you show respect for their wisdom and experience?

Remember That Family Is Vital

Native American families—like families in most cultures not too far removed from an age when survival meant depending on one's family—are traditionally close. Each member is valued. In the past, how that family and the individuals within that family conducted themselves could have dire consequences for the tribe. Native American families tend to value diversity. Each member of the family is important. Each should be respected and listened to. Each sees from a different perspective, and we need all perspectives.

The Harmony Way consists of both a sense of unity and diversity that recognizes an individual not just for how they can continue the family's survival but for their uniqueness and giftedness. The focus is on the good of the whole, and each individual is a part of the whole. Everyone is necessary.

Increase your friendships and family.

15

BALANCE

Working Hard and Resting Well

Two Cherokee stories help us understand work and how it relates to the Harmony Way. Kanati and Selu are the First Man and the First Woman of the Cherokees. *Kanati* means "the Hunter," and *Selu* means "Corn."

The Hunter and Corn Mother had two sons. One son was Home Boy, their biological child. The other was Wild Boy, who had been found living in the canebrake along the river. This story tells what happened when the sons were nearly grown and Selu's husband, Kanati, was away, in the West.

One evening, Selu saw her sons getting their weapons ready so they could go out to hunt the next morning.

She smiled and said, "I see you're going to hunt tomorrow. When you come back, I'll have a wonderful meal prepared for you."

The next day, while her sons were gone, Selu took all the older meat, cooked it into a soup, and thickened it with hominy grits. In the evening, the boys came back with a deer they had killed, and their mother served them this soup. They thought it was very good and ate eagerly, but they didn't know what it was. They had never seen or tasted grits or any type of corn before. "This is selu (corn)," their mother said, "and it's very good food."

The next morning, the boys went out hunting again. This time, their mother took fresh venison, cut it up finely, and once again thickened the soup with hominy grits. That evening, the boys returned with two turkeys they had killed. Once again, they enjoyed what their mother had prepared very much.

The next morning, as they were leaving to hunt, Wild Boy said to Home Boy, "This corn our mother gives us is a very mysterious thing. Where does it come from? Let's spy on our mother to see where she gets this." Creeping back through the woods, the boys watched as their mother came out of the house with a large basket. They saw her go into a shed, and they quietly ran up to peek through the cracks in the shed wall. They watched as their mother placed the basket on the floor of the shed. She then struck her sides and rubbed her belly. Corn, from which she made the hominy grits, fell from her body, filling the basket.

Home Boy turned to his brother and whispered, "This is a very disgusting thing we've been eating."

"Yes," Wild Boy said, "and it looks as if our mother is a witch."

That evening, the boys returned from the hunt with no game. Their mother had worked hard preparing the turkey meat with hominy grits, but the boys only picked at their food. They didn't eat.

Finally, their mother broke the silence. "Something is wrong," she said. "Maybe you have learned something. Maybe you don't like what I have prepared for you. Maybe you don't like me anymore."

One of the boys said, "We know where the corn comes from. We think you are a witch. We have to kill you now."

"Do as you must," their mother said, "I ask only this one thing: When you have killed me, drag my body over the ground seven times in each direction as far as you can go. Wherever my blood touches the ground, a plant will grow. This plant you will call selu (corn). You will take care of it, and it will take care of you and feed you. As the stalks grow, they will form ears. You may pick some ears when they are green, for roasting or boiling. They are very good. The rest you must allow to get ripe and hard. This you will use for hominy and to make your bread. Don't forget to save the best for seed. As long as you have this corn with you, you have me with you. I am Selu, the Corn Mother."

And so the boys killed their mother. They dragged her bleeding body over the ground. But they were lazy and only dragged her around three times in each direction. Wherever the blood touched the Earth, corn grew.

The people had food to eat. But because of the original laziness of the boys, the corn must be hoed each year. The women wisely took over the management of the crops.

The companion story to this one describes the two boys, in disobedience to their father, following him to a cave. There they discover that Kanati's work each day—bringing home wild game for them to eat—means simply going to the cave and calling for an animal to come out. Then he would simply close the cave and return the next day for another animal. So the boys come along after Kanati and accidentally let all the animals out of the cave.

In both stories, those who listen come to understand food as a gift from Creator. There are ceremonies and even festivals that accompany planting, harvesting, and hunting rituals, which formalize our gratefulness to Creator. Kanati was able to simply go to a cave to hunt one animal at a time. Selu was able to pull corn right from her side. Food is a gift, these stories tell us.

After the children's disruption of the Harmony Way, however, it became much more difficult for them to find game and produce food. Hunting became a chore for the Cherokee men and growing vegetables was hard work for the women.

The idea of Corn Mother sacrificing her body also shows that to retain the balance of Harmony Way, we must sacrifice our labor and skills to work for our food.

These two stories about First Man and First Woman encourage Cherokee men and women to work, through gardening and hunting, to keep the harmony. The stories urge them to maintain the accompanying ceremonies and rituals. Among our Cherokee people, women planting and men hunting is what contributes to making us Keetoowah. In most of the seven Cherokee festivals, corn is used and honored as that which gives us continual life.

Work, within a Native American worldview, must have a purpose, and it must be related to present needs. The Western worldview related to work is remarkably different from the Native American worldview.

According to several studies set forth by Professor Jerry Mander, contemporary Americans work far more hours in a day than Native Americans of the past ever worked. He asks the question of modern Americans: "So, have things really improved? Those of us who enjoy the fruits of the techno-logical juggernaut have more stuff in our lives. . . . But if we compare ourselves to preindustrial societies, it is arguable that we work harder than they did. In addition, our devo-tion to gathering and caring for commodities has created an extraordinary modern paradox: a scarcity of time, loss of leisure, and increase of stress amidst an environment of apparent abundance and wealth. A decrease in the quality of life and experience."

We turn in this chapter to notions of work and rest, and balance. How does our work lead toward or away from harmony? Why is work meaningful, and what does it accomplish? When have we done enough, and how will we know? What would it look like to work hard and rest well?

Cultivate an Open Work Ethic

An open work ethic is important to mention here as an aspect of the Indigenous value of balance in life. Native Americans have traditionally viewed work as purposeful and to be accomplished as needed. This means that Native American values concerning work are more about meeting a present need than about gaining future wealth, power, and material possessions.

As we saw in chapter 10, when we looked at Native ideas about time, it is not that future needs are not considered but rather that the present need is the immediate concern. The future will be taken care of when future need arises.

Like all agrarian and nomadic peoples of the past, Native Americans have had to plan for the future in order to survive. That Native Americans lived in cooperative communities also meant that it was not up to each individual person to worry about supplying everything needed for their future. In this sense, the value of work and the value of community overlap. An open work ethic means we work to meet our needs and the needs of our loved ones, but that we don't let work become the be-all and end-all of our existence and identity.

Native American values concerning work were traditionally role oriented. This was especially true concerning male and female roles. Historically, in Cherokee society, the young boys learned hunting skills by guarding the cornfields from nighttime scavengers. As they grew older, they progressed to hunting with their male relatives in the mountains. When they became young men, they were eligible to go on faraway trips for big game and even war parties. Among the Cherokees, men hunted and went to war, although Cherokee society, like many other Indigenous societies, allowed for exceptions to role assignments. Men brought home wild game, and women dressed and cooked it. Women planted in the fields and harvested the food. While most tribes in North America are no longer agrarian or nomadic, some of the role ideas are still common today.

Do Not Overwork

To overwork—that is, to spend time working for what one does not need—means that one's life is out of balance, and it breaks the circle of harmony. The idea of working primarily as needs arise may have developed throughout ancient times. Creating surplus or degrading the environment are frequent results of overwork, and neither made sense in a traditional Native worldview.

It is common knowledge among Indians to avoid contacting tribal offices early on Mondays or late in the afternoon on Fridays. Even if their hours state they are open, the staff might not be there. The joke that goes around Indian Country, especially as it applies to those working for the tribe, is that Indian employees have Mondays and Fridays off.

The humor is found in that among many tribes, some employees either come in late or not at all on Mondays, and on Fridays, they are absent or leave early. The most common reason is that they are traveling to attend distant pow wows, which generally begin on Friday evenings and last through Sunday late afternoons. Other reasons for missing Mondays or Fridays include hunting and fishing seasons, going to weekend wakes or funerals, attending ceremonies or Native American church meetings, and visiting relatives. Most of these are considered reasonable and respectable absences by the tribes.

The general ethos creating this value is that one should work as needed. Overworking creates the very real possibility of missing out on life. Work is valued among Native Americans as a necessity, but to overwork is foolish. Overwork creates a great opportunity for the clowns to tease us back into harmony.

To Native Americans, the time and work categories of the dominant culture are arbitrary and usually don't fit with Native American lifeways. "Indians often become frustrated when the work ethic [of the dominant culture] is strongly emphasized," reads one manual on Indian education. "The practice of assigning homework or in-class work just for the sake of work runs contrary to Indian values. It is important that Indians understand the value behind any work assigned, whether in school or on the job."

What values are connected to the work you do? Where do you find yourself tempted to overwork? How can you resist messages from wider culture to overwork?

Connect Your Work to the Work of Others

I (Randy) enrolled in my doctoral program with several other Native American colleagues. We discussed our decision to pursue our degrees with great consternation. How could we spend all this time and money pursuing something for our own personal benefit? How could we make sure that our studies connected to our people?

We finally decided that each person would concentrate on a slightly different area of study in order to better help our Indian people. One of us would study a particular discipline, one of us another discipline, and so forth, so that together we'd be learning different skills and knowledge that we could share.

During the orientation to the graduate program, then, all the new students were asked to discuss, among other things, why they were pursuing postgraduate studies. All the other students gave reasons that had to do with their own personal career goals: their desire to teach, their longing to write, their hopes to do a particular kind of research. Each of their reasons was about themselves.

When it was our turn, we Native American students talked about the great need among our Indian people to advance so we would be taken seriously in the academic world. My Native peers and I spoke of how our studies and degrees would open doors for our Indian people that would not otherwise be open to them. None of us talked about personal goals. We talked about what we wanted our work to do for our community.

During the tough times ahead of us—difficulties that inevitably emerge during graduate studies—each of us could draw strength, in our individual studies, from our identity and commitment to our friends and our Indian people as a whole. We supported each other as we sought that education, and we committed to using it in a way that would benefit our people.

What if we all saw our work as a way to participate in and benefit a group rather than serve our own individual purposes? There's a strong sense of harmony that comes when we work together.

Defy Traditional Categories of Employment

Native American unemployment figures are often difficult to determine. One early study of Native Alaskans suggested they viewed wage jobs as something they could do in *addition* to other, more traditional tasks and methods; the researchers found that "significant numbers of Native Americans chose to work intermittently in the wage economy." Subsistence hunting, sharing of resources within the community, nonmaterialism, and other factors led the researchers to be uncertain about how to categorize employment. The researchers concluded that this ambiguity, however, "may reflect the actual vagueness of unemployment among individuals who maintain a lifestyle combining economic activity in both the modern and traditional sectors in the context of extended families who provide mutual economic support." It is perhaps unrealistic to expect that precise answers to questions on unemployment can be found in this cultural context.

One interpretation of this study's findings might be simply that certain categories of Western thinking do not fit Native Americans. What those researchers realized is that the same cultural categories used to measure the dominant American culture do not apply to Native American culture. Their findings depend on what one means by *unemployment*. Here, community values concerning sharing come into view. When everyone is pitching in and sharing resources, each individual does not need to work every day. Native American views of freedom also comes into view here.

How might we free ourselves from the constraints and categories of work imposed on us by colonialism and capitalism?

If Native American spirituality is primarily concerned with maintaining harmony in cooperation with creation, Creator, and others, it does not make sense to overstock unneeded food or resources. Hoarding means both depleting natural resources and creating a storage problem. Neither does it make sense to hoard food away from the needs of others. Additionally, if Creator is seen as the supplier of food, it might seem presumptive and ungrateful to take more than one needs. When all these components are considered, and when we act in deference to one another, there is harmony and freedom from worry.

Reject Materialism

Materialistic values of Euro-American modernity are very different from our own Indigenous values. "The Puritan work ethic is foreign to most Indians," writes one author. "In the past, with nature providing one's needs, little need existed to work just for the sake of working. Since material accumulation was not important, one worked to meet immediate, concrete needs. Adherence to a rigid work schedule was traditionally not an Indian practice."

Generally speaking, Indians are not materialistic. Materialism and consumerism are values imposed on Native Americans. The differences between Native North American values and those of the dominant society have been noted throughout our mutual history. Ronald Wright, author of *Stolen Continents*, writes of this conflict between settler and Native American understandings of wealth: "The problems were those which arise wherever a stable, collective system and one based on expansion and individual profits collide. It was, for instance, impossible to run a store or plantation profitably without violating the way of reciprocity fundamental to most Amerindian societies. To obtain respect in the Native world, people had to redistribute wealth; for esteem in the white world, they had to hoard it. To a Cherokee, sufficient was enough; to a white, more was everything."

"More was everything": what an apt description of the culture that surrounds us. And "sufficient was enough" gives us a window into Indigenous perspectives on consumption.

The Cherokee concept of redistribution of wealth was at direct odds with the individualism of settlers. Until the nineteenth century, the Cherokees were able to retain their communal values. Remember: this was even *after* removal from their homelands. For a people to hold on to cultural values during times of extreme oppression, including forced relocation, is remarkable.

After touring Indian Territory in 1887, Senator Henry Dawes described the Cherokees in this way:

> The head chief told us that there was not a family in the whole nation that had not a home of its own. There is not a pauper in that nation, and the nation does not owe a dollar. It built its own capitol . . . and built its schools and hospitals. Yet the defect of the system was apparent. They have got as far as they can go, because they hold their land in common. . . . There is no selfishness, which is at the bottom of civilization. Till these people will consent to give up their lands, and divide them among their citizens so that each can own the land he cultivates, they will not make much progress.

"Progress," according to Senator Dawes, meant individualism, materialism, and even selfishness. None of these ideals are Cherokee values, nor do they represent the values of other Native Americans. He was unable to see that the

Cherokees were operating according to an entirely different worldview.

Native Americans are not immune to hard work. In fact, some of the hardest-working people we have known are Indigenous. But in order to maintain a life of harmony, there must be a balance between work and rest, or recreation.

Work hard and rest well.

16

GENEROSITY

Sharing What You Have

Constant visiting among friends and relatives is a hallmark of Native American communities. No one should be left out, and no one ever goes away hungry. Complete strangers are often given special honor and gifts at pow wows and other social functions as acts of generosity and welcome.

In fact, maybe the worst thing one can say about an Indian is that they are selfish. Generosity is an unspoken but foundational rule for life. There is also an insistence that no one should be alone. Alone, people have no protection. Alone, people have no fellowship. Alone, the tribe or clan does not exist, and harmony cannot therefore exist.

Hospitality and generosity, both requiring others, are the natural economy in the Harmony Way.

We turn our attention to the Indigenous value of generosity, which often looks like hospitality and welcome. Anthropologist Carl Starkloff notes the historic practice of hospitality among Native Americans:

> On reading the various accounts and monographs by explorers and anthropologists, what strikes one is the almost universal hospitality shown by Indian tribes, especially to their White visitors. It is quite remarkable as described in David Bushnell's writings about explorers and missionaries among the Siouan, Algonquian, and Caddoan tribes west of the Mississippi. . . . There are practically no examples of inhospitality or harsh treatment rendered to Whites. On the contrary, the tribal leaders went out of their way to receive these visitors as special guests. There seems to have been a conviction among the Indians, at least until the middle of the 19th century, that they and the newcomers could share the land equally, even if the land was sometimes thought to be the tribes' sacred inheritance.

That statement is a long way off from the savages of the American myth. There were practically no examples of inhospitality because hospitality is central to living in harmony. One could not be greedy or inhospitable and remain in balance.

Give Your Best to Others

We were taught by Randy's Kiowa father that any gift you give from your heart is a good gift. He also taught us that among the Kiowa, if someone compliments you on a piece of jewelry, a hat, or some other object you value, then it is your obligation to give it to them. And you must give it to them without begrudging the act. Gifts among Native Americans are an act of the heart, regardless of their monetary value. The practice is an exercise in nonmaterialism.

Giveaways are a common practice throughout Native communities in the United States and Canada. Native Americans in the Northwest have a similar practice called a potlatch. We have observed giveaways in many places with only slight variations. Basically, a giveaway is a formal public ceremony in which an individual or family gives away any number of items to others. The giveaway items may be expensive or not, and they may be personally valuable or not. I have seen horses, saddles, rifles, baskets, blankets, and many other gifts given. They may even include sacred items, such as drums or eagle feathers. The gifts may be given to strangers, friends, elders, those in need, or other honored guests, but, as we were taught, they are not supposed to be given to one's relatives.

The one thing that all giveaways have in common is that items are given *by*, and not *to*, the person who is being honored. In other words, in many Western cultures the person of honor—the one who has the birthday, or the anniversary, or the graduation—gets the gifts. In giveaways, the person of honor *gives* them. The idea is that it is the privilege of the person being honored to give things away. The honored person shows generosity by sharing his or her honor with others in this way, thereby spreading the honor around.

Giveaways are routinely done at certain times in Native American culture: entry into the pow wow arena, the making of a chief, the giving of an Indian name to a person, and other celebratory occasions. We had giveaways at our wedding, when our children entered the pow wow arena, for each of their coming-of-age ceremonies, and other occasions.

Although the giveaway is a formalized method of generosity, the spirit of generosity pervades Native American communities. And it can pervade your life too. How might you create a giveaway in your own life?

Give Quietly

There is a place in the Indian community for public ceremonies, such as a giveaway. There is also a place for more subtle, quiet giving.

We have seen people give without any recognition. Sometimes a guest has left a gift in our home during a visit—a gift we only notice later after they have left. We have seen straightforward and unencumbered giving, as when a person simply extends their hand with a gift and expects nothing in return except perhaps a handshake. We have also observed occasions when acts of kindness are done for someone in need, especially for elders. Many times no one knows who did the kind act: leaving boxes of food on a person's porch, cutting wood for the winter, and cleaning yards. We've seen all these acts without anyone knowing who expressed the generosity. What all these forms of secret or quiet giving have in common is simple generosity from the heart, without fanfare or expectation.

Invite Friends and Strangers for Feasts

The most formalized and, quite frankly, the most beautiful demonstration of generosity and hospitality in Indian Country we have observed is during the Pueblo Indian Feast Days. Each of the nineteen Pueblos has its feast days at different times from the others, and some even do this twice a year. We have been fortunate enough to attend two different Pueblo Feast Days.

On these days, everyone in the village cooks their finest meals, and then they open up their village to strangers and invite all to have a meal with them.

We have enjoyed these feast days immensely, and we can say without a doubt that this act, and the spirit it creates, is an impressive and moving example of generosity. People save for months ahead of time to make sure they have enough food to share for the feast. Many of the people are living with little means themselves, and yet they take great pride in feeding absolute strangers the best meal they could imagine. The food we experienced on such occasions was unbelievable.

Originally, before colonization wiped out many of the villages, there were over one hundred Pueblo villages. If each of these feasts was spaced out at different times, that means any stranger would have access to food every three to four days or so. In this way, the generosity of feast days is not only an incredible act of hospitality; it is a huge safety net for the most unfortunate people in their society.

We both were taught how to be generous and hospitable by example from our parents. I (Randy) remember a time when I was a teenager, alone at our house. A knock came on the door, and when I opened it, I found a short, rotund fellow standing there in overalls covered with mud. He was rough-shaven and spoke with a definite country accent. "I'm a homeless feller, and your daddy told me if I ever needed food to come on by," the man said. I greeted him, asked him to come in, and went about filling a grocery bag full of canned goods. I gave him our can opener and the makings for a fresh salad. The man took the bag and left.

When my parents came home, they found the bag on the back porch, still full of food. I explained what happened, and my parents were proud of my generosity. Still, we were all baffled by who the man was and why he hadn't taken the food.

Later that day I heard my mom and dad laughing and talking to someone on the phone. It turns out it was my dad's second cousin. He was a pig farmer, and he had no need for food. He was pulling a practical joke on me because I did not recognize him as my dad's cousin.

We had a good laugh. Yet there was a more serious test in the interaction. What will we do when someone shows up on the porch or at the bus stop or in our community with a need? Will we rise to the occasion, or will we turn them away? If in our community some are well fed and others are going hungry, no one is in harmony.

What might it mean for you or your household or your community to prepare food and even feasts for strangers or those in need? What might the value of hospitality require of you?

Give When You Have a Lot—and Also When You Don't

We can think of many occasions when we were not prepared to have guests in our home. Most of our years were spent living paycheck to paycheck—and often those paychecks came months later than our employers promised. Like many people, we learned how to live on a tight budget.

But what do you do when you have few groceries and no money and someone shows up at your house for a visit? In our understanding of the Harmony Way, you share whatever you have. On those occasions, our elders' teachings about sharing what we have with others hit us before we could panic or complain.

One time a family of seven from back east showed up at our house unexpectedly, and they wanted to stay for several days. We had only a few hours to prepare for their arrival, and with those few hours of warning, we called for all hands on deck. We mustered up what little food we had, ran to the store, charged what was needed, and planned out the meals.

More recently, a group of six Native Alaskans showed up at our house for an unexpected visit. We had such a great time talking and visiting that, before we knew it, it was time for supper. With elders present, we knew we had to find something nourishing to feed the group—and quickly. We had a large pack of hot dogs left over from a recent event. We threw together all the cans of various kinds of pinto beans we had, and we ran to the garden to gather lettuce for a salad, which was the only vegetable in season at the time.

These are the times when you just make do with what you have. Generosity doesn't have to look like a lavish occasion or a perfectly executed meal. It just has to look like love.

Share what you have.

EPILOGUE

Life Is a Circle, Not a Straight Line

As we come to the end of the book, we want to make sure you do not leave with the impression that the journey to Eloheh is easy. The Harmony Way might sound enticing, but it is often seen as a threat to the current order of things. Many people are invested in and benefit from the way of disharmony, domination, and dispossession.

Here we return to a bit of our story. While we were living in Nevada in 1998, I (Randy) had a dream that changed our life direction completely. In the dream, I saw Native people and others in the modern world who were living and flourishing at a special place. There was a farm, and there was a Cherokee mound in the middle of the place. There were no cars, and everyone walked everywhere. There was also a place of ceremony and a school, and it was a living community. It was a serene place, a place of peace and harmony and contentment. It was like nothing I had ever seen or imagined, and it felt so real.

I woke up Edith and shared the dream with her. We cried together as we realized the sacred vision at the center of the dream. It was Eloheh! As days and months passed, we began to realize that following this dream—a dream of Eloheh for our people and others—was to be our life's work.

Actually *realizing* the dream? Now that would be another story.

After moving away from Nevada in 2000, we landed near my parents in Alabama as a home base. We spent four years on the road while building a support base for the Eloheh vision, mentoring others, and speaking. We home-schooled the three kids from a van as we drove across the United States and Canada, averaging about sixty thousand miles a year. Visiting reserves and reservations throughout Indian Country was a wonderful education for the kids. All the while we were sharing the vision with others and looking for that special place in my dream to make the vision of Eloheh come alive.

Periodically we would take off to Cherokee Country and look for the place. After years of some extremely time-consuming and discouraging dead ends, we were finally given support and encouragement to purchase land in Kentucky, seven miles south of Nicholasville.

Thus began Eloheh Village. The land was incredible: fifty acres of wooded hills and meadows, with a large creek running along the edge. With donor support and many volunteers on the ground, we made progress toward a place of Eloheh at breakneck speed. Within two years we had developed springs and wells; built fenced pastures, corrals, a barn, and a staff cabin; and had several other families, including Native American elders, living there all or part of the year.

We also had horses, cattle, sheep, goats, chickens, ducks, and gardens, and we had planted two orchards. We were actually about 75 percent self-sustaining at that point. We were also running extended weekend schools held on the land. Our schools were very successful, hosting thirty to forty students each session and centering on the Harmony Way. We had built bunk rooms in the garage and over the garage. But there was so much interest in learning about Eloheh that we still lacked room. People slept on our couches, on our floor, in the yard, and sometimes in their cars. It was a good problem to have. Our living room seemed to be shrinking with each school.

I had been working with the county to get approval for seven small KOA-type sleeping cabins and a central building where we could meet. In April 2006, I attended a county planning meeting to get final approval for our cabins. To my surprise, the room was full. I thought to myself,

"Someone here must have something controversial on the agenda." Little did I know that it was *us*!

Unknown to us, our neighbors, who had never been friendly, had been meeting together for months, planning how to stop us from holding our schools and building the buildings. Nine of them testified against us. Here is a sample of what they said at that county meeting:

"Everyone knows Native Americans are drunks. They will wander on our property and get hurt, then try to sue us for everything we have."

"Who is going to protect our children from these people? We will need to hire more police and all our taxes will increase."

"Schools should be in town. There's no reason a school should be out in the country."

"These people here seem to be all right, but the ones coming from the reservation: we just can't have that."

"I hear they want to be self-sustaining. That's admirable, but it's all clay-based soil, and you can't grow anything in that. Next thing you know they'll be starving, and the government will need to ship free food to them. We can't have them big trucks on these little roads!"

That night we were denied our permits, which was extremely disappointing. Then, a few days later, some of our neighbors—who we found out later were White nationalists—set up a fifty-caliber machine gun right on our property line. They commenced firing it at all times of day and night.

Things got much more serious at that point. We kept the kids inside the house, and we began to fear for our and our animals' lives. The sheriff told us he couldn't do anything to stop them. They were on their property, and they were firing on their property. They had a permit for the gun. They were only trying to scare us, he said—which they did.

In our prior work, we had fought injustice at universities, cities, counties, and major corporations. But this was too much. It was not worth an accidental ricochet and someone getting killed. The sheriff, the state's attorney general, the Fair Housing Council, and the Justice Department were unwilling to step in and help us. We were on our own.

We decided to take a week to pray and think this through. We landed at a friend's place in northern New Mexico. Though it was heartbreaking, we eventually decided that wisdom and safety called for us to move once again. The dream of Eloheh was dying.

When we put up the "For Sale" sign on our property, the machine-gun fire stopped, but the persecution didn't. Our kids were threatened at school by the various neighbor kids. While we waited to move, we decided, for safety's sake, to transfer them to the public school system on the other side of the county, which meant driving them back and forth fifteen miles every day.

After building up fifty acres into a real farm and school, having a major influence among Native American people and others interested in Eloheh, we were being forced to give up the dream. Unfortunately, the national economic downturn hit about the same time. No one was buying houses—especially houses with fifty acres. We had to refinance twice over the next two years in order not to lose the place. Finally, we were forced to sell it all at under half its appraised value.

After losing everything, we crossed the continent and attempted to replicate the original vision on a small farm in Newberg, Oregon. The farm in Newberg was only 3.5 acres and had severe zoning restrictions. We did the best we could with what we could afford at the time, fixing up the ninety-six-year-old home and farm, which had not been a farm in over twenty years.

Nine years later, we were finally able to create what was the original vision for Eloheh, in Yamhill, Oregon, not too far from our farm in Newberg. Now, at the time of this writing, we have been here just over three years. We live on ten acres we call Eloheh Indigenous Center for Earth Justice and Eloheh Farm & Seeds. Once again, we began a new farm from scratch, and our schools have resumed. You can read more about that venture in the next section.

Final Words for the Journey

There is a better way of living in this troubled world, and it is a way that Indigenous people have known about from time immemorial. It has less to do with the pursuit of happiness and more to do with finding harmony with the whole community of creation. And as we have often found in our own lives, it threatens the competitive, consumerist version of the pursuit of happiness.

True well-being is rooted in the Harmony Way. The happiness that so many pursue will simply disappoint. Rather, the good life, at least for us and hopefully for you, will be found in the ten Indigenous values we have outlined in this book:

- Seek harmony.
- Respect the sacred.
- We are all related.
- Look forward by looking back.
- Laugh at yourself.
- Speak from your heart.
- Listen to everyone.
- Increase your friendships and family.
- Work hard and rest well.
- Share what you have.

We want you to discover and walk your own personal journey toward living in balance and harmony. Living the Harmony Way will look different for you than it does for us, and we do not claim to be experts. We have given these things much thought and research, and we have tried to live out the way of Eloheh. We do not speak for other Native Americans, including even those we mentioned or quoted in the book who spoke for themselves. We speak only for ourselves. But our sincere hope is that you, through understanding a bit about our experiences, will be able to find the inside and outside paths of the Harmony Way for yourselves.

A common mistake that people make is thinking of the journey to Eloheh as a straight line—a movement from one place to another, with clear steps and no detours or loops. But remember that in chapter 7 we discussed the idea of imagining harmony as a hoop, not a line. The Harmony Way is actually a sacred circle. You can enter the circle at any point to begin your journey, and the circle is continuous.

Like us, you will likely find yourself going back to these values at various times in your life. You might find that your vision of Eloheh progresses in fits and starts. You might discover that it threatens those who are invested in systems of disharmony.

But if we can leave you with any wisdom for your journey, it is this: living out the Harmony Way is worth anything it might cost you. It is the way that we as individuals and societies can back away from the precipice of self-destruction. In the sacred circle of life we continue to learn, apply, and mature in our practices. Eloheh is not a philosophy but a lifeway. As these values become a reality in our lives, and as we learn and relearn them, we move in the sacred circle, and we support each other.

We wish you well on your journey. We continue on ours!

—*Randy and Edith Woodley*

ABOUT ELOHEH

Eloheh Indigenous Center for Earth Justice and Eloheh Farm & Seeds focus on developing, implementing, and teaching sustainable and regenerative agroecological Earth practices. While there is an identifiable farm within the almost ten acres near Yamhill, Oregon, the whole property is considered vital, including wildtending, as part of the farm. We have created a center that embodies educating our whole selves in the context of the whole community of creation to fulfill our mission of living in harmony with the land, using North American traditional Indigenous knowledge (TIK), wisdom, and practices as a guiding model.

We are a 501(c)3 nonprofit under the auspices of Eloheh/ Eagle's Wings, which began in 1999. You can find out more about our work and connect with us at https://www. eloheh.org/.

We welcome people to come and join us in this work. The last Saturday of each month, from March through October, are scheduled volunteer work days and an excellent time to become acquainted with our life's work. Visitors may sign up on our website (the days last from 9 a.m. to 3 p.m.). Many of the people who have visited us have now become friends and family. Our seed company is doing well, and farming takes up a lot of our time. We sometimes take on interns. We also host extended weekend schools at various times as well as six-week online cohorts. To stay tuned, sign up on our website for our monthly email blasts.

Mostly we host people and share from our hearts. That seems to be good enough. After they leave, people send us many dear words of thanks for connecting them with nature and a renewed sense of spirituality. We hope that they are finding their own way toward harmony and well-being in the places where they live.

Together, in this place, we are journeying toward Eloheh. Maybe we will see you here sometime as well?

NOTES

Chapter 1

"In a little more than one hour": Cotton Mather, *Magnalia Christi Americana: Or, the Ecclesiastical History of New-England* (1702), as quoted in Howard Zinn, *A People's History of the United States: 1492–Present* (New York: HarperCollins, 2003). However, it's worth noting that while Zinn attributes the sentiment to the general Puritan viewpoint of the time, the exact quote may not be a direct citation from Cotton Mather's works. Instead, it may be a paraphrasing or a representation of the broader sentiment held by some colonists regarding the Native Americans.

This is the myth: John C. Mohawk, *Utopian Legacies: A History of Conquest and Oppression in the Western World* (Sante Fe, NM: Clear Light, 2000), 260.

Chapter 2

Mental health professionals are seeing: For more on climate anxiety, see "Yale Experts Explain Climate Anxiety," Yale Sustainability, March 13, 2023, https://sustainability.yale.edu/explainers/yale-experts -explain-climate-anxiety.

"The furnaces of the world": "Coal Consumption Affecting Climate," *The Rodney and Otamatea Times*, August 14, 1912. An even deeper dive reveals that the text of this news item has its origins in the March 1912 issue of *Popular Mechanics*, where it appeared as a caption in an article titled "Remarkable Weather of 1911: The Effect of the Combustion of Coal on the Climate—What Scientists Predict for the Future."

The term "greenhouse gases": Svante Arrhenius, "On the Influence of Carbonic Acid in the Air upon the Temperature of the Ground," *Philosophical Magazine and Journal of Science* 5, no. 41 (April 1896): 237–76, https://www.rsc.org/images/Arrhenius1896_tcm 18-173546.pdf.

The advent of the Anthropocene: Will Steffen, quoted in Joseph Stromberg, "What Is the Anthropocene and Are We In It?," *Smithsonian Magazine*, January 2013, https://www.smithsonianmag.com/science-nature /what-is-the-anthropocene-and-are-we-in-it-164801414/.

He chooses the term Eurocene: "Jairus Grove Response to Jedidiah Purdy," January 4, 2016, *Boston Review*, https://www.bostonreview .net/forum_response/jairus-grove-response-nature-anthropocene/.

"Women must see": Rosemary Radford Ruether, *New Woman, New Earth: Sexist Ideologies and Human Liberation* (New York: Seabury, 1975), 204.

A future where women lead the way: Vandana Shiva, https://en.wikiquote .org/wiki/Vandana_Shiva.

The United Nations did a study: Nafeez Ahmed, "UN: Only Small Farmers and Agroecology Can Feed the World," Permaculture News, September 26, 2014, https://www.permaculturenews.org /2014/09/26/un-small-farmers-agroecology-can-feed-world/?fb clid=IwAR3DRoNE7JosDXgcXUqe4_BLrufrEqMCsuxPPIW7S SfazqlQ6DnbOzLkHI.

According to the Biomimicry Institute: "What Is Biomimicry?," Biomimicry Institute, https://biomimicry.org/what-is-biomimicry/?gclid =CjwKCAjwm4ukBhAuEiwA0zQxkyD1ZIgLhNTBz9R8ULAq

Chapter 3

No one knows for sure how many: For more on the Indian residential schools in the US, see the website of the Federal Boarding School Initiative, https://www.bia.gov/service/federal-indian-boarding -school-initiative.

Chapter 7

When Euro-Americans hear statements: As a teacher of Native American history and culture, Randy has heard this argument from his Euro-American students dozens of times.

"Even the most severely eroded Indian community": Vine Deloria Jr. and Daniel R. Wildcat, *Power and Place: Indian Education in America* (Golden, CO: Fulcrum Resources, 2001), 43.

"A translation of mitakuye oyasin": Clara Sue Kidwell, Homer Noley, and George E. Tinker, *A Native American Theology* (Maryknoll NY: Orbis Books, 2003), 51.

"The teachings are very good": Paul Wallace, *The Iroquois Book of Life: The White Roots of Peace* (Sante Fe, NM: Clear Light, 1986), 14.

"In explaining the good news": Wallace, 108–9.

"Today, we should use": Edward Benton Banai, *The Mishomis Book: The Voice of the Ojibway* (Hayward, WI: Indian Country Communications, 1988), 9. "Banai" is an honorary title bestowed on traditional Ojibway spiritual leaders. They are also referred to as Gichi Dowan, meaning "Big Medicine people."

"There are yet more teachings": Benton Banai, 113.

"The image of living on the Earth": James Treat, *Native and Christian: Indigenous Voices on Religious Identity in the United States and Canada* (New York: Routledge, 1996), 54–55.

"The Indians of the American imagination": Vine Deloria Jr., *God Is Red: An Indian View of Religion* (Golden, CO: Fulcrum, 2003), 23.

Revered Brule' Lakota Chief Spotted Tail: Don Trent Jacobs, *Unlearning the Language of Conquest: Scholars—Indianism in America* (Austin: University of Texas Press, 2006). 135.

"Sweet Medicine advised": Stan Hoig, *The Peace Chiefs of the Cheyenne* (Norman: University of Oklahoma Press, 1980), 7.

Decentralized, multilevel peacemaking efforts: Randy has been taught all these things by Cherokee elders and friends at various points in his life.

"These two people were an influence": Randy's dissertation, a conversation with Adrian Jacobs. See "The Harmony Way: Integrating Indigenous Values within Native North American Theology and Mission" (PhD diss., Asbury Theological Seminary, 2010), 108.

Doctrines asserting original sin: In his studies as a theological scholar and historian, Randy came to understand that the Christian church created a charade of salvific control over others by developing a false doctrine of human sinfulness via one's nature and the false doctrine of hell, which was meant to scare people into submission to the church.

"Bravery is to face challenges": Taiaiake Alfred, *Peace, Power, Righteousness: An Indigenous Manifesto* (Don Mills, ON: Oxford University Press, 1999), 134.

Chapter 9

"Is there a human being": Brian Edward Brown, *Religion, Law, and the Land: Native Americans and the Judicial Interpretation of Sacred Land* (Santa Barbara, CA: Greenwood, 1999), 38. (Testimony of Jimmie Durham, at Tellico Dam Congressional Hearings, 1978. The Sixth Circuit dismissed the Cherokee claim to prevent flooding of Cherokee sacred sites and villages.)

"With one mind": "Haudenosaunee Thanksgiving Address Greetings to the Natural World," National Museum of the American Indian, 1993, https://americanindian.si.edu/environment/pdf/01_02 _Thanksgiving_Address.pdf.

"Only now, son, are you ready": Randy Woodley, *Living in Color: Embracing God's Passion for Ethnic Diversity* (Downers Grove, IL: InterVarsity, 2004), 156–57.

Chapter 10

"This religion as revealed to me": William A. Young, *Quest for Harmony: Native American Spiritual Traditions* (Indianapolis: Hackett, 2002), 149.

"The structure of their [Native American] religious traditions": Deloria, *God Is Red*, 65–66.

Chapter 11

"Human beings are often weak": Peggy V. Beck and A. L. Walters, *The Sacred: Ways of Knowledge, Sources of Life* (Tsaile, AZ: Navajo Community College, 1977), 30.
"Fundamentally, the sacred clowns": Beck and Walters, 307.

Chapter 14

The report argues that lack of social connection: "Our Epidemic of Loneliness and Isolation 2023: The U.S. Surgeon General's Advisory on the Healing Effects of Social Connection and Community," Office of the US Surgeon General, 2023, https://www.hhs.gov/sites/default/files/surgeon-general-social-connection-advisory.pdf.

Chapter 15

Americans work far more hours: Jerry Mander, *In the Absence of the Sacred: The Failure of Technology and the Survival of the Indian Nations* (San Francisco: Sierra Club Books, 1991), 254.
"So, have things really improved?": Mander, 254–55.
"Indians often become frustrated": Arizona Adult Literacy and Technology Resource Center, *Teaching and Learning with Native Americans Handbook*, 1996.
One early study of Native Alaskans: Judith Kleinfeld and John A. Kruse, "Native Americans in the Labor Force," *Monthly Labor Review* 105 (July 1982): 50.
The researchers concluded that this ambiguity: Kleinfeld and Kruse, 50.
"Puritan work ethic": Quoted in Woodley, "Harmony Way," 230.
Conflict between settler and Native American understandings: Ronald Wright, *Stolen Continents: Five Hundred Years of Conquest and Resistance in the Americas* (New York: Houghton Mifflin, 1992), 207.

Senator Henry Dawes described the Cherokees: Scott L. Malcomson, *One Drop of Blood: American Misadventures of Race* (Darby, PA: Diane, 2000), 15.

Chapter 16

"On reading the various accounts": Carl Starkloff, *The People of the Center: American Indian Religion and Christianity* (New York: Seabury, 1974), 88.